Your True Colors:
Power Up and Heal with Color Psychology

Inspire your brand, app, interior design or personal appearance,
by developing your Color Sense and understanding how color affects us all

**TEN YEAR EDITION EXTRA
5 INDIVIDUALS' COLOR CODES**

Catherine Shovlin

Also by Catherine Shovlin and available on amazon / kindle / other bookstores

- **Live Life in Full Color: Power up and heal through your chakras.**
- **Walking Through Walls: Proactively challenging barriers in ourselves and society**
- **Sacred Death: Reclaim dying, Embrace living** Overcoming our fear of death, dying and grief to enhance our lives and support each other
- **Author link** books2read.com/CatherineShovlin
- **Website:** windsofdiscovery.com

Published by Windsofdiscovery.com

Table of Contents

Introduction

A word from the author

Thank you for buying this book from Winds of Discovery. I have enjoyed writing it in London, Bali and Umbria over the last few months and hope that you enjoy reading it.

I would like to dedicate it to color guru Angela Wright, who led me into this extraordinary world when we first worked together in the 1990s on changing the red and yellow of the Shell logo. Since then I have used these principles many times, working with color primarily as part of marketing and branding projects or space making, both in my own strategy and research consultancy, and in association with Patricio Forrester in Artmongers.

Thanks also to all the friends and family who have encouraged me on this venture and to Linda and Jane for reading and offering such intelligent observations.

Catherine Shovlin, London 2014 and Sydney 2024

The Color Sense approach

We do not live in a black and white world. Color impacts our mood, our well-being, our energy levels, and our appetites. In every environment, in any outfit, under any source of light we are reacting to color cues whether we realize it or not. As Carl Jung, a pioneer in the field of color psychology said, "Colors are the mother tongue of the subconscious". This book will help you access some of that information and discover how that knowledge can help you at work and in your personal life.

In this book we will explore how color psychology affects us and how we can learn to work with it to our advantage, tuning up your Color Sense so you can create the atmospheres and reactions that are most relevant to the situation. I hope your experience will open your eyes to color and the powerful role it plays in our world - whether we see it or not - and give you new sources of pleasure as you revel in color and thrive in your own true colors.

Despite the impact of color on our decisions and states of being, color psychology is a relatively young science. What you read here might chime with your personal experience and make immediate sense to you or you may notice gradual changes in your awareness of color.

Lastly, a word about the aim of this book. You will see it is in five sections after this introduction.

- Part One – Why Color Matters: will give you some insight into how color psychology works affects our lives and why it is worth understanding it to feel more comfortable and get better results by optimizing color palettes.

- Part Two – Your Color Sense will help you understand the workings of color psychology and develop your own Color Sense
- Part Three – Applying Color considers the impact of color schemes in three important areas: interior design, branding, and our personal wardrobe / appearance. You might find it interesting to look at all three or focus on the section most important to you.
- Part Four – Individual Color Codes. 5 examples of how I created the Color Code for each person based on their unique skills and attributes.
- Part Five - Conclusions

If you follow the exercises at the end of each section, you will build your Color Sense as you go. You may be surprised by how far that goes beyond the 'red and yellow makes orange' color information we have all grown up with.

Some additional references to training and resources are given at the end of the book for those who wish to delve more into the concept and its practice.

Just to prepare you I'm going to let you into a secret before we start. We don't just see colors with our eyes. You may be surprised at how much the exercises focus on other feelings and senses. You will be developing your Color Sense somatically - with your whole body - as well as tuning up your instincts in this area. Enjoy the journey.

Color shapes our life

From the early stages of our evolution as humans color has had an important role to play in our survival. For example, we instinctively shy away from yellow and black stripes - nature's way of saying watch out.

This has been reflected in the built environment and whoever first came up with the idea of yellow and black stripes on road signs was responding to a deep-seated reaction to the color combination. We, in turn, have been trained both by nature and by traffic signs to beware.

Most of us are drawn at a deep level to an expanse of green, experiencing a sense of peace and safety based on years of foraging.

And you can probably make a reliable guess about what is meant by "blue sky thinking" even if you have never heard the term.

We may also share the sense of excitement, enervation and maybe overstimulation that comes from seeing many colors and shapes together

In the days before sell by dates and refrigeration, a good understanding of color could have made the difference between life and death. Identifying the right berries or fungi and not eating the meat that was beginning to turn were vital skills and the tendency for food gatherers to be women may account for the fact that even today they tend to have measurably greater color discernment than men.

Color blindness is also much more prevalent in men - those early hunters would primarily have needed to detect movement and focus on their prey so color discernment would have been less of an evolutionary requirement than focus, strength, and reaction speed.

Over the millennia these specialization trade-offs have become reflected in our species and are in part accountable for those conversations between couples where she can scarcely believe he thinks that shirt goes with that sweater or the debates I have with builders starting by them saying "but it *is* light green, what's the problem?"

Shaping our world with color

So how can we increase our understanding of color and use that Color Sense to our advantage?

I hope you will find this book relevant on both a personal and a professional basis. To help you develop your Color Sense you will find exercises at the end of each section. I encourage you to read the book in stages, maybe only a section a week, and practice the exercises in between so you can feel your color awareness growing as you progress through the book. I can share information, but only you can develop your own skills.

This book will not make you a technical expert on color. There is a lot of science in the field and in the final section I suggest some places you can go if this interests you.

The technology of creating a color that looks the same in a textile, in print and on your smart phone is extensive and complex. You may be fascinated by that and want to find out more or you may be intrigued by the mathematics and physics behind color, or the biology and chemistry of how we see it.

What I hope you get from this book is a stirring of your Color Sense. You may well have a natural aptitude for what you are going to learn here - the fact that you have been drawn to this book in the first place suggests this could well be the case - or you may find it more challenging.

Color awareness is a physical skill more than an intellectual one. It feels more like learning to drive or roller skate than learning algebra. And like those skills you will grow your Color Sense over time.

Much of what I know I learnt from Angela Wright - a pioneer in the field who has devoted her life to understanding color psychology and its impact as well as sharing her knowledge widely with the aim of increasing color harmony in the world. See the end of the book for more resources.

Whether you are planning a new corporate look and feel or deciding what color to paint your kitchen, from the color of your knickers to the color of your report, this book will show you how to develop your ability to tune in to the power of color. And shine in your true colors.

Part 1: Why color matters

Impact of color psychology

In this first part of the book our focus is on knowledge. What is color psychology all about and why might knowing more about it be helpful?

From early childhood we have been aware of color. It is thought that babies first notice black and white, then red, and subsequently the rich range of colors most of us can see. Our personal journey of color follows the evolutionary journey of color naming that is seen repeated in languages all over the world.

If you have looked after a baby, you may notice it seems more relaxed in some environments, bedding or outfits than it is in others.

As preschoolers our parents and carers usually teach us names of colors, a piece of information that can then become so automatic that we barely give it a thought. In kindergarten and at school we start to learn how to mix colors and achieve the effects we want. I have a vivid memory of frustration that no matter how much white I put in a jar of red poster paint it showed very little inclination to become pink. I was astonished when I was shown how just a few drops of red turned the jar of white paint the color I was after.

Nowadays you might be used to color specifications for computers (RGB) or printing (CMYK) or paint (JAL). You might have argued with friends and family about whether that cushion is light green, leaf green or lime green even though any one of these includes many variations, they are labels not firm definitions. So, let's find out more about what is going on.

Science of color

If you are curious about the science behind color or would like to understand how something works, then read on. If you are happy to just accept that it matters and more interested in what to do with it then you could skip to Chapter 3: Noticing color.

Color comes to us via light waves. You probably know how shining a pure white light into a prism causes it to diffract into many colors, each at a slightly different angle. When we see an object as red, in fact it is absorbing all the colors of the spectrum except red which is reflected back and therefore visible to us.

Light waves are part of the electromagnetic spectrum which also includes for example radio waves, microwaves, and X-rays. They are emitted by objects and the shorter the wavelength, the smaller and hotter the object which emitted it.

So, the colors of the rainbow range from longer wavelengths like red (just a bit shorter than infra-red) up to shorter wavelengths like violet (just a bit longer than ultraviolet).

If you were subjected to radiation you would expect to be physically affected and the same is true of light rays and therefore color. Not with the same extreme effects as gamma rays but with some impact.

In fact, in experiments with seeing and non-seeing individuals, response to color is very similar. So, although we primarily relate to color in a visual way, in fact it also generates a physiological reaction - which is where a lot of the importance of color lies.

EXERCISE 1 - color awareness

During the next few days, you may at times be in environments with a large expanse of a single color. At this stage we are not differentiating between shades so although, for example, a field of wheat has many colors in it, the overall sense of golden expanse is what we are focusing on for now.

This color might be in nature - a field, a lake, a cliff face - or it might be in the built environment such as a feature wall, a vehicle, or a basketball court. Whenever you notice a lot of one color, pause for a moment, breathe it in.

Try not to over analyze but just notice if anything in your body feels different. Look away for ten seconds and then back to the color you were focusing on. Again, breathe and notice. You might want to jot down any reactions and see what patterns emerge over the next few days.

At the end of the week, review what you have observed and see if any patterns or hypotheses have emerged.

Maybe you have a particular relationship with a particular color - a strong memory, either positive or negative, or strong cultural reasons to prefer or dislike it.

Our reaction is layered - as well as the instinctive reactions explained in Chapter 3, you will have your own unique cultural and personal layers of reactions. See if you can learn to distinguish between them and notice what is going on for you.

When you start to choose color later in this book it will help if you know what your personal reactions are or specific to your cultural references and what are more widespread reflections of the human condition.

Reflections

What did you notice?

How consistent were your reactions?

How would you separate your reactions into:

- physiological impacts e.g. calming, exciting
- cultural effects e.g. sophisticated, festive, feminine
- other factors e.g. fashion, your mood

Keep your notes from this and future exercises, your first steps into developing your Color Sense. You might want to go back to them and add further observations as you deepen your relationship with color and its impact.

The physiological impact of colors

Although the field of color psychology is a young one, it has much older roots of study.

In 1798 Goethe and Schiller developed the "rose of temperaments" which used color classifications and the concept of the four humors to identify likely occupations as shown in the table.

Type	Colors	Suitable Occupations
Melancholic	Crimson, purple	Philosopher, pedant, ruler
Phlegmatic	Blue	Public speaker, historian, teacher
Sanguine	Green	Hedonist, lover, poet
Choleric	Yellow, Orange	Tyrant, hero, adventurer

Part 1: Why color matters…The physiological impact of colors

If you practice yoga or meditation, you may already be aware of chakras - energy centers - in the body and their associated colors. This ancient knowledge shows some relationships to Goethe's work.

More recently, experiments have been conducted where subjects are blindfolded and placed in a room. When a color wash is projected onto the walls, various physiological measurements are taken to see how they are affected by the color of the light. From these experiments we now know scientifically what color experts have been saying for thousands of years; that different colors produce different effects on our body.

You can probably think of several examples where color is used in relation to our physical or emotional state and you can see the correspondence here. Seeing red, green with envy, yellow belly - these saying reflect our folk wisdom about color and how we connect to it.

So, let's take a quick tour of the main colors.

Red

Experiencing the color red increases heart rate - our body clock - which therefore gives us a sense of time passing more quickly. All our reactions get speeded up as our body readies itself for fight or flight.

Just think how useful that would have been when moving fast to avoid a deadly snake or frog. Or to react to the sight of fire, fever, or blood. Nowadays that same reaction helps us react to road signs or eat fast and leave fast in a typical fast-food joint.

Physiologically, red is the color our eyes see first, which accounts for its high level of impact. It is unusual to find product packaging that has no red at all. Interestingly it is also the first color to be named in the evolution of most languages (after light / dark which are the first two distinctions that are made).

Red is also a color we associate with anger. As well as raising our heartbeat, red has the effect of raising the testosterone of the wearer and lowering that of the onlooker.

That makes the red team more likely to win than the blue team in physical activities[1]. Given this testosterone effect, it is interesting that shown the same photos of the same women wearing red or blue, those in red win on seeming to be more attractive.

This is such a powerful factor that it works even when the dresses can't be seen! So, if you are female, although red may not be a great choice for a job interview (it does not give the impression of high intelligence for example) on a hot date, it might be just the job.

This may well be a response to the fact that redness is associated with increased blood flow and healthiness so the

____

[1] See Hill and Barton's paper on the subject for more information on the impact of red in combat sports

blushing bride may be a safer bet for producing children than the paler ice queen. Whatever our conscious intentions in the dating game, these underlying evolutionary biology drivers still play an important role.

It is interesting to notice how color reactions creep into our idioms. Red mist, seeing red and red-hot all evidence our relationship with this color.

Yellow

Yellow also has its physiological effects and is known to increase endocrine activity, heightening emotion, and emotional reactions. So that famous round, yellow, smiley face emoji may cheer you up even more if you are already in a good place… or give you a sinking feeling if you weren't feeling so good in the first place. This increase in emotional reaction, sometimes described as our gut feelings, is likely the origin of yellow being attributed to cowardice.

Of course, feeling afraid in a terrifying situation, or reluctant to cause injury to others e.g. during a war, is entirely normal and human. The process of recruiting soldiers to create an army needs to find ways to overcome this natural reaction so identifying these human responses as cowardice - yellow belly - or lack of patriotism is one way of encouraging individuals to overcome their instincts.

In terms of chakras, yellow is associated with the solar plexus (sunshine yellow?) and some popular sayings reflect this relationship between courage / fear and this part of the body - butterflies in our tummy, having the guts to see it through.

The practice of painting nurseries yellow when the gender of the baby is not known doesn't make a lot of sense given this information. Most parents would want their baby to feel calmer not more emotional when they put him or her in their crib to sleep.

Similarly, when working in a mental health hospital earlier this year I was surprised to see that the de-escalation room, a place where overwrought patients are sometimes placed for a period to calm down, was also painted yellow. That was an easy fix, but it made me wonder how many times that mistake is repeated throughout similar institutions all over the world.

Blue

Another important reaction to be aware of is that blue increases mental activity. Now that blue sky thinking makes more sense, doesn't it? The shade and intensity of the blue affect how this reaction manifests.

So celestial blues and a sense of light and openness encourages creative and lateral thinking, while dark ominous blues can suggest authority and thinking in the form of rational structures like protocol or discipline. It's a smart choice then for police uniforms and airline pilots.

In research tests, blue has been identified as the preferred color for brainstorming and creative thinking, whereas red is better suited to problem solving when urgent fixes are required. Blue tends to encourage more forward thinking and a tendency to think through the whole process, not just the first step.

Some studies have shown that blue can improve results on cognitive tests[2] where red does not. Blue school uniforms could make sense then. Unfortunately, the standard navy blue used in schools is not appropriate for many students and may be counterproductive by making them feel drained or too restricted. As the role of education changes in our evolving society it will be interesting to see if there is an organic shift towards schools that encourage learning rather than conformity.

Green

In our early days as humanity, life originated in the horn of Africa at a time when there was a reliable food supply. As climates changed early man and woman had to travel further afield to find food security. Small wonder then that we are hardwired to react positively to the sight of acres of green. It means there is a good water source, that there is probably food, and that animals are also likely to thrive, giving us hunting opportunities.

---

[2] See Andrew Elliot's work on this subject for more details

Part 1: Why color matters…The physiological impact of colors

Years ago I took a photo of plants growing in Ethiopia during a famine where new approaches to agriculture and water management were of critical value. These were indeed green shoots of hope.

As our early ancestors extended their territory away from the tropics and into temperate areas with seasons, green shoots signaled the end of the winter or the dry season. The hope of spring and new beginning brings a surge of optimism and wellbeing even today despite 24-hour supermarkets in many countries offering permanent food security - though maybe the response to a heap of greenbacks (US$) echoes that deeply held reaction.

It's interesting that green was traditionally used in hospitals - what better place to encourage a sense of healing and well-being? Over time that shade of green also has associations (see chapter on Cultural References) but the original idea was intuitively correct, the psychological effect of green is a calming one inducing a sense of universal acceptance, peace, and wellbeing.

White

In contrast, when our ancestors saw a white landscape that was unlikely to mean good news. A barren snowy landscape could mean a long hungry winter - or during the ice ages, a need to relocate to survive.

We are fortunate that evolution has taken us well past this dependency on hunting and gathering firsthand, but we still have an instinctive reaction to this lack of abundance and associate whiteness with sterility, scarcity, minimalism, and purity.

Our eye is instantly drawn to a small speck of color in a glass of milk as our ancestors would have had a sharp eye out for the occasional berry or plant that had survived the cold.

Psychologically, white is more about absence than anything else. So, while it makes sense for the medical profession (cleanliness, absence of germs or contamination) it was a poor choice for UK Job Centers in the 80s, especially as it was combined with orange which as we see next, stimulates appetite. Making people want more then reminding them of their lack is an unhelpful combination.

Orange

With its combination of red - creating a sense of urgency - and yellow for emotions, our physiological response to orange is an increase in appetite. That might be in the most obvious form of hunger, or an appetite for sex or material goods. A zest for life has an obvious relationship here.

Orange creates a sense of need and longing - just flick through a traditional cookery book and you will see that it is the predominant color, from golden pastry to roast chicken to peach tart.

It can be found in Mexican restaurants but can be a little too vibrant for northern European tastes, creating anxiety with its strong energy and making it a 'hot' but less common color in the fashion world though, like red, a dash of orange can have a powerful energizing effect on an outfit or room scheme.

Purple

Purple is associated culturally with prestige and psychologically with spirituality or a higher level of existence.

Close to ultraviolet on the electromagnetic spectrum it is a portentous color whose sense of luxury was reinforced during the Middle Ages when in Europe only royalty were allowed to wear it - hence the term royal purple.

In today's world it is often used by products and services offering either luxury or the possibility of enhanced spirituality due to its high vibrational frequency. In chakra terms it is the highest chakra, above the crown of the head - on Maslow's hierarchy of needs it would be around self-actualization.

Black

Black is not so much a color as the total absence of light. In our everyday lives we do not often come across complete darkness - there is usually some ambient light pollution, but the thought of total blackness in a cave or in outer space can create a heavy sense of deep-seated fear. Our instincts are on high alert because anything could be lurking in the dark and it will be up to our non-visual senses to save us.

Black signifies heaviness - the densest stones are black - which makes it an unfortunate color choice for those feeling self-conscious about their weight. Despite this fact, black is very often worn by many of us, including those who would rather weigh less and tends to be seen as a safe option in the sense that it is unlikely to provoke a reaction (as opposed to the red dress effect we saw earlier!). This is a correct assessment, but black will also not be doing us any favors unless it is a good color for us personally - see Part 2 for more information on choosing personal colors. For the rest of us, the little black dress itself may look great, but it will make us look drained or tired.

This quick tour will have given you some idea of how color impacts on our lives. Not merely in an aesthetic sense, not only because it is this year's 'in' color but also because our subconscious responds to it and creates physiological reactions. Whether we like it or not. Developing your Color Sense will allow you more choice about these reactions, in yourself and in others you wish to influence, which you may find beneficial.

EXERCISE 2 - color distinction

Most of us are drawn more to some colors than others and may have no hesitation in declaring our favorite color - blue being the most popular choice in the West.

However, since the human eye can discern millions of colors it is interesting to explore the more subtle nuances of color.

Start by picking a generic color (e.g. red or blue rather than scarlet or navy)

Over the next few days collect as many examples as you can of that color. That could be scraps torn from magazines, food packaging, pieces of clothing, scraps of cloth, cosmetics, paint, flowers, leaves, stones… anything that catches your eye and is your chosen generic color. Try to get at least 10 examples.

Now spread them out and look closely at the color. As well as being lighter or darker, each one will also be a particular shade. For example, if you picked green, some may be yellowish green, some blueish green, even some reddish green.

Organize your examples according to the rainbow from left to right (red, orange, yellow, green, blue, indigo, and violet) and from top to bottom with lightest at the top and darkest at the bottom.

By undertaking this exercise, you are starting to see color more subtly. Green is not just green.

It is worthwhile starting to keep some color notes for yourself. Even just a simple system of a drawer of color references like those you have gathered in this exercise and a notebook of your reactions to colors and contexts is a good start.

Part 2: Developing your color sense

Noticing color

If you did the last exercise, you have already started getting your color muscles in shape. The more you notice the color around you the more your Color Sense will develop and the easier it will be to distinguish, recognize and classify different colors.

Of course, unless you have issues like blindness or color blindness you will have been seeing colors all your life. What we are talking about now is moving to a more somatic (body based) way of seeing and feeling colors that will give you skills to use color with confidence, subtlety, and a clear intention.

If you carry out the exercise at the end of this chapter you will be further strengthening these color muscles and you may start to notice your Color Sense increasing. First, I want to introduce three other factors to bear in mind.

Balance

An important aspect of color is the balance between different colors. We are instinctively reassured by good color balance and it creates a sense of well-being. When corporate logos do not have this, they feel a little unstable - or as though they are missing something. You don't need to be a color expert to notice this - research has demonstrated the difference by asking respondents to rate fictional logos according to trustworthiness. The results confirm that those with color balance feel stronger and more reliable.

By 'balanced' I refer to the primary colors, the presence of red, yellow, and blue in some format. This doesn't mean the primary colors have to be in every color scheme, rather that they are a component of the colors being used - in the way that blue and red are present for example in lilac.

The effect of color balance can be felt in a room. Have you been in spaces where the color scheme is monochromatic? Maybe an extremely pink bedroom or a grey lounge. It can feel a little stifling and one dimensional. Yet add an attuned green to that pink room (so red, yellow, and blue are all present) or an orange cushion to the grey room and suddenly the dynamic is quite different. When identifying a color palette for a space, or any other application, have balance on your checklist of things to consider.

Harmony

We will examine this subject in more depth in Chapter 7, but for now let us rely on your natural instincts - and develop them further in the exercise at the end of this chapter. A sound starting principle is that nature is in color harmony. And because we are part of nature, we respond to that rhythm. The way some notes clash and sound discordant the same is true of some colors. As with music, it may sometimes be an intended effect to create uncertainty and even anxiety in the audience, but in many more applications color harmony is a more productive aim.

Think of this as the effect of combining for example pretty alpine wildflowers with tropical blooms. It just wouldn't feel right - the tropical flowers will make the delicate Alpine ones look washed out and flimsy while tending to look overly brash themselves. By putting each type of flowers in a setting that is in harmony they will show at their best.

When colors are in harmony, our deepest reactions, the ones that have been with us since the early days of our evolution, know that things are more likely to be all right. We don't need to be on guard. Engineers use the maxim that if it looks wrong it probably is. The same response, based on years of our own experience and millennia of genetic memory, is true for color.

So, while it is entirely appropriate for an art installation to use clashing colors and unexpected combinations to challenge the viewer, it is less helpful to do the same in a hospital waiting room or a bank logo. In these situations, and many others, we wish instead to reassure the person experiencing the environment or the brand, to give them a sense that this is something that can be relied upon, a space where they can relax and trust the provider.

CASE STUDY: Children's Neuroscience

In St Thomas's Hospital, London, children on the autistic spectrum and with other neurological conditions come from a wide catchment area for assessment and identification of a treatment program.

After travelling for a few hours, experiencing the fast pace of London's public transport system or the frustration of city traffic, the young people and their parents or carers are unlikely to arrive relaxed. Add to this the high stimulus environment of the children's hospital in St Thomas's - great for a typical child with a broken arm but over-stimulating and stressful for those on the autistic spectrum

By the time these children and their families saw a therapist they could be extremely agitated, distressed or behaving badly. Our aim was to create an environment in the new ward for these children and their carers that would be more conducive to a calmer state where assessment and therapy could be more productive.

A large part of that project was a series of ten artworks built into the environment and an important starting point was defining the color palette. Working closely with the clinical staff we developed a color scheme based on light blue, soft green and beige. The calming colors were a peaceful backdrop for the artworks and worked well with the rounded furniture that was developed, creating a space to breathe rather than a stressful waiting environment. The overall creative theme was wind in its many forms including weather, science, and the feeling of wind.

Color harmony throughout the space helped smooth the journey from the waiting area to the treatment rooms.

Metamerism

The third aspect of color that we need to consider is the impact of colors on each other. You have probably seen this optical illusion demonstrating the effect on our visual perception of changing the combination of colors.

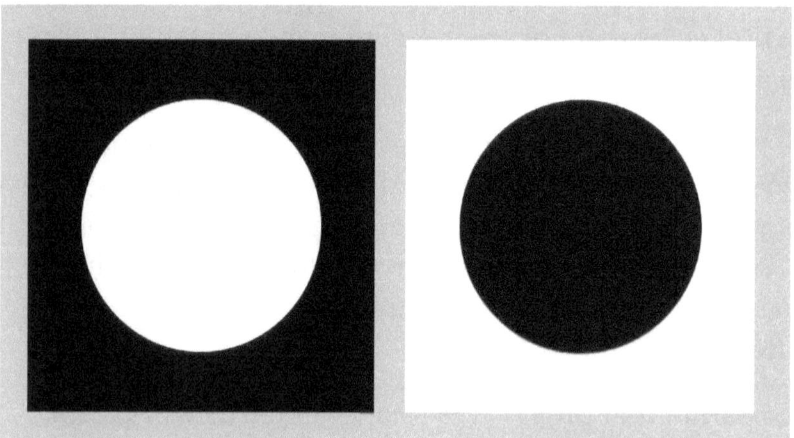

And if you try taking three photos of the exact same plant against different color backgrounds you will be able to observe differences in the plant. Changing the field – the surrounding color - changes our experience of the object. Context is important.

So, when we are considering colors for an environment or even an outfit, we need to bear that in mind. This is particularly important if you want to maintain consistency for a corporate logo. Remember that it will look quite different against different color backgrounds (and terrible against some that are not in harmony) so make sure you define the acceptable conditions clearly in your brand guidelines and give the right amount of space around the logo to allow it to flourish.

EXERCISE 3 - color harmony

Again, this is an exercise that works best if you do it over a period of days.

- Start to notice the combinations of colors in your environment. You may want to pick something specific like a magazine cover, a shop interior, or a favorite view.
- Consider what you have chosen from the three points of view we have considered in this section - balance, harmony and metamerism.
- Does the color balance feel right to you? Does it have an appropriate energy level for the environment and the purpose it is serving? If so, see if you can identify exactly why and if not, what do you think might help? You don't need to "know" the answer at this stage, by trusting your instincts you are helping them to strengthen.

- Now color harmony. Do the colors sit comfortably together? If not is that for deliberate effect or is maybe a mistake based on lack of Color Sense? Can you see which colors would need to be removed or changed for them to click into place? Sometimes the change is not dramatic - a less forceful pink maybe or a slightly grayer shade of blue. Play around in your imagination to see what feels right.
- And lastly metamerism. Is this working well and making some colors pop and draw attention in an intentional way? Or is it adding confusion to the color story?

Living in color

In our everyday lives, our subconscious is observing color all the time. It is constantly scanning our environment for things that might matter enough to alert our conscious brain.

That's why if you have just bought a red mini car, you suddenly see red minis everywhere. Logically you know they didn't just appear overnight, it's just that they are now relevant so your subconscious has tagged them as an object of interest. You might have had the same experience when you are in love - you keep thinking you've seen the other person in a crowd, even if you know they are thousands of miles away. Your subconscious is tagging any signs that someone it knows you consider important is in the vicinity.

Usually most of what we see is screened out by our subconscious - but we do have some choice in the matter. As you develop your Color Sense it is common to start to find more pleasure in color. That flash of koi in a blue pool. The sunlight shining through leaves. The multitude of tones in your baby's skin or lover's eyes. Relish it and know that as well as bringing you pleasure that noticing it is also increasing your ability to discern colors and, later, to harness the power of color.

To develop your Color Sense further I will suggest a few exercises you can have up your sleeve for odd moments in the day. Because this is a process of raising awareness as much as it is about learning facts, you may find they come easier to you on some days than others. Rather than ticking off an exercise as done, try incorporating and repeating them as an ongoing practice and see what you notice about your deepening Color Sense.

EXERCISE 4 - tuning into color

We all have moments in the day when we are in an environment without needing to be mentally active. Maybe your bus to work, the supermarket queue, sitting in a coffee shop, walking the dog.

Next time you have a moment like this pick a color - you could try working your way through the rainbow during the week - and be alert to it. Let's say you pick red. For those few moments just notice red. That sign over there. That fire extinguisher. The label on someone's bag or jeans. You will probably have the experience that the tiniest scraps of the color you are now tuned into pop out and catch your attention. You may be surprised at just how many there are.

As well as improving your Color Sense, this is a good mindfulness exercise that will pull your attention into the present moment.

Observing use of color

After this introductory information you are now able to start noticing color everywhere you go. You will also start to notice times when the color feels a bit off and it's good to guard against the negative feelings this can induce. The aim of this book is not to create color tyrants! You may find the exercise at the end of this section a useful counterbalance to all the examples of 'bad' use of color that you are going to start noticing.

By now, what you have learnt may also be starting to affect the colors you choose to wear. I know some people who have to dress very soberly for city jobs but choose their underwear carefully depending on the main task of the day. Need that extra bit of power in the boardroom? Make it a red knickers day. Need some creative strategic thinking at that workshop this afternoon? Time for the sky-blue underwear.

If you work in a less formal environment you may be able to be less discreet but some caution may still be required - remember it is not just the color itself that has an impact but also the amount you wear and the degree to which it is expected in that context. When I first started working, I had a range of outfits which meant that maybe once a fortnight I wore a tailored orange skirt. After only a few months I became aware that I was being described as 'the woman who wears orange' as though it was an everyday occurrence. I then realized that although it was only an occasional choice, I was in fact the only person who EVER wore orange, thereby making it a very noticeable choice.

This kind of situation may work to your advantage or not - it's up to you to decide what to do with the knowledge and how and when you want to stand out or blend in.

EXERCISE 5 - color emotion management

If you find yourself getting riled by color abuse, then a grounding exercise can be to just notice one color that works or feels good in each situation. You can do this sitting on the train or bus or maybe in a queue.

Just work your way round the carriage (trying not to stare too obviously). For each person congratulate them in your head for one color they are using that you think, or feel is a good idea e.g. 'Those green socks give you a certain lightness of being', 'the pink stripe in your scarf brings color to your cheeks'.

The more you do it the more fluid it will become.

This exercise is working on multiple levels. Of course, it is raising your Color Sense by flexing those color muscles to give you more confidence in your ability to see color and know when it is right. You are also gathering many examples of the positive potential of color.

These will build up your experience and make it easier to know what is right when you are starting with a blank sheet of paper. And lastly it will probably improve the overall atmosphere on the train or bus as you are subtly giving each person a little positive attention. Whether they know it or not this will improve their well-being a little.

We are never going to be in a world of perfect color harmony unless we are in a purely natural environment - and those are few and far between. So rather than becoming distressed by the "wrong" colors, you might choose to find joy in the "right" ones that you come across.

Color psychology theory

Color harmony

Color harmony is a significant aspect of working with color. It is rare that a single-color choice is made in isolation. Much more commonly, it is part of a bigger picture.

Experiments have shown that our reaction to color harmony is intuitive. And in most cases the required impact is to reassure and give confidence rather than to create a sense of uncertainty and risk. So, knowing how to achieve color harmony is an important skill for any color practitioner.

Angela Wright explains in the <u>Wright Theory</u> how there are four groups of colors within which color harmony is guaranteed. Once you have identified which of these four Color Groups is more appropriate to the environment, enterprise or individual it will become much easier to select the right colors for the job.

When I first explain this to graphic designers I have worked with, they tend to be somewhat appalled. They immediately fear restriction and lack of creative expression.

In fact, those who work with the Wright Theory quickly come to realize that the restriction is minimal - after all if we can see millions of colors then that means there are plenty for each of the four Color Groups - and creativity can often be enhanced by the thinking space created by the definition of the right color family.

A profound advantage of identifying the most appropriate color family is it takes a lot of subjectivity out of the debates around logos, publications, or physical environments. It is no longer a question of personal preference - rather it is a case of selecting what works for the job that needs to be done.

CASE STUDY - color match

In a branding workshop I split the people there into ten teams. Each team consisted of a Client and a Creative Department of three people. The person roleplaying the Client was interviewed by the Creative Dept.

The brief was the same for each team - come up with a poster to advertise a soft drink. Each team had access to the same materials - colored pens, colored paper, and images.

By asking a few carefully chosen questions, and without any other training, the interviewer identified the Color Group that the client was most likely to belong to. The clients then left the room and the creatives used the color palette and design principles of the Color Group to create a poster.

They also did a language profiling exercise.

At the end of the exercise, all ten posters were put on display side by side and the clients were asked to come back into the room. They viewed the posters and each of them went to stand next to the one they felt was the most persuasive, the most likely to make them want to buy the soft drink. 8 out of 10 of them stood by the poster that had been designed specifically with their color and language preferences in mind. The remaining two were very similar to each other so interchangeable.

This compelling result makes a strong case for the power of getting color right. If you only had one client for your soft drink and you had the chance to talk to them, you could profile them and tailor the packaging exactly to them. But what about the more usual situation where we have multiple clients? Or – equally - multiple patients, students, employees, or users. They all have a choice about how they react to the stimulus they are shown, whether that is advertising for products, your staff website or a doctor's waiting room.

So, let's say your target audience is everybody coming into the emergency room or your new clothing store. You can't interview each client and redecorate just for them so what can you do? The good news is there is a solution, and we will look at this issue more closely in Part 2 of this book - how to choose colors in various situations with a focus on three areas: environments, brands, and personal use of color.

First though, let's first focus on improving your ability to sense color harmony. In the coming week, keep an eye open for this aspect. Start by noticing the combinations of colors you see around you now.

EXERCISE 6 - awareness of harmony

How comfortable do they feel? At first, your own color preferences might be the strongest factor, but over time you will develop your Color Sense so you can feel where there is color harmony even if it is not among colors that you like.

For example, you might not like red at a personal level, but is it working in this situation? Is this tone of red in harmony with the colors around it? Maybe you can start to tell what would help. Red might be a good idea in this situation but maybe a stronger red would work better, or a pinker one. Try imagining the other reds in this context and see if you can find one that feels like it fits.

Be aware while trying this exercise that many color combinations you look at will not be in harmony. Some may have been purposefully put together by someone who understands, or who has good instincts, for how these things work and is aiming for a particular kind of impact. But many will clash because of the - often accidental - way in which the environment has evolved; a patchwork of years of decisions by different people, maybe without any consideration of color.

Try not to get overwhelmed by the jumble of colors you will be seeing. Just take a breath and consider whether the colors are in harmony or not. Is this an easy fix? (E.g. swap out those sage green napkins for grass green ones) or is it just too much of a muddle of different Color Groups so it's hard to know where to start. As I said earlier, the aim of this book is not to create color tyrants and sometimes we just have to accept the things we cannot change.

As you develop your Color Sense, you may experience increased discomfort when you are in a space where the colors are not in harmony. Or looking at it another way, there is plenty of scope for improvement out there!

If you have any say in the environment, you might want to experiment with some changes and then revisit this exercise.

The four Color Groups

As I explained in the previous section, the most important thing when creating a space, a brand, or even an outfit is to maintain color harmony and work with colors from a single Color Group. If this is achieved, the result will have integrity, confidence, and credibility. So how do you decide which Color Group is the right one to use?

For now, the general principle we will apply is to identify the Color Group most appropriate to the role and personality of the situation (the waiting room, the shop, the corporate brand…) and then select colors within that Color Group that do the job required, using the information you have from earlier around the physiological and psychological impact of different colors.

Choosing the right Color Group though is where the real skill comes in. To be able to do this reliably takes proper training and I recommend the courses you can find at the Colour Affects website. I'd like to give you some idea though so let's take a quick look. For each of the four Color Groups I have described the technical aspects of the colors, the personality traits associated with them and how they can be undermined.

This last point is worth a little more explanation.

When we are presented with a range of colors - say in a color advertisement, an interior design, or a logo - the best reaction will be if the colors are from an appropriate Group for the product or context and *all from the same Group*. When this isn't the case, the colors will undermine each other. This is the most common handicap of color schemes - that they undermine themselves.

Learning to tell for sure will take you months and maybe years of training, but at least being aware of the problem may raise your ability to notice it. You may find yourself thinking - that looks a bit heavy or this feels a bit flimsy - these are triggers for you to consider if a lack of harmony may be the problem.

Lastly you will see in a moment that the seasons are one way used to describe the four Color Groups. In this case I have used the single seasonal cycle taken of temperate zones - namely spring, summer, autumn (fall) and winter. If you live in a different climatic rhythm, it might be interesting to consider what would make a good equivalent naming system in your local environment.

The finger test

When I was first learning about colors, we were given a batch of colors to take home and sort into Color Groups. Once I had covered the kitchen table with small squares of color, my daughter, who was about six at the time, got interested. I explained the exercise to her and showed her how I had sorted them but wasn't sure of all of them. Let's see, she said, and closed her eyes.

I was just about to explain that we had to look at the colors to decide when I realized what was happening. She was running her finger over pairs of colors and *feeling* if they were in harmony or not. As I saw her sort colors into what felt like much better groupings, I tried it myself.

It might work for you too. As you run your finger across the boundary of the two colors you may feel nothing, or you may feel a kind of buzz. In most cases, for me at least and maybe for you, the buzz indicates the colors are not in harmony. It's worth a try!

EXERCISE 7 - Further color harmony

You can build your Color Sense without leaving home. Try flicking through a magazine and tearing out a few adverts. Full page ads are great because of the way they are designed. Sort them into three piles - the ones that feel in harmony to you, the ones not in harmony and the ones you are not sure about

Keep the "not wanted" clothes in a pile, maybe with a blank piece of paper on top so you don't get distracted by their energy. And spread out the ones that feel in harmony - considering them will help you get more accustomed to looking at harmony and knowing it when you see it. After doing this for a day or two, have another go with the clothes you deemed "don't know". Is it any easier to place them now?

Is your Color Sense improving?

Working in this way should help you to feel more confident in your instincts. When you really can't decide visually about harmony, try the finger test, and see if that gives you more information.

Group 1 (spring, morning light)

In some systems this first Group might be referred to as spring or morning colors, and much of their personality is in tune with those times of the day and year. They are warm, light, clear and sparkling like fresh dew. If you look at the Pantone reference you can check that there is no K (black) in the mix as this would create muddier colors that do not belong in this Group.

The personality traits associated with these colors are a high degree of sociability, extroversion with a charming twinkle.

These colors are light on their feet, quick to catch on - and just as quick to move on. Aficionados will love the fun and lightness these colors bring. They are quick-thinking, charming communicators with a sharp wit and flirty approach. You often see colors from this Group in products targeted at the so-called girl market - hen nights with pink limos and pink champagne, sweet sixteen parties. Of course, politically this does have some challenges - is the implication that girls are just for fun?

Products in this Group are sparkling with clear, light colors - not just pink. They may be decorated with crystals or silver filigree. Design shapes that work well for these colors include bubbles, starbursts, and floating shapes with a lightness and airiness in the design.

If undermined by being combined with other Color Groups, these colors can seem flighty, lacking in substance or gravitas. But used well they can have a lot of accessible appeal.

Group 2 (summer, daylight)

This Color Group - also sometimes referred to as daylight or summer colors, is easiest to imagine if you think of a languid English summer rather than a tropical version. Elegant women drift by in swathes of lavender and sage, wisteria droops against a well-worn wooden arch and conversations are soft and murmured. Shapes are soft and flowing - nothing dramatic or angular. Colors are cool, muted, and gentle.

The personality traits are in tune with this scene. A peaceful elegance and serene confidence. Not flashy or pushy, just quietly and meticulously getting everything done. It may seem effortless but there has been plenty of attention to detail behind the scenes.

In terms of applications, you may see these colors in up market boutiques aimed at older women, in paint ranges recreating the English country house look or in a spa.

These are not colors for the hard sell but rather for the discerning customer who already knows their own mind and doesn't need drama to make their mark.

If undermined by colors from a different group, these colors can seem weak and wishy washy, rather too mannered or polished for some tastes and somewhat aloof.

Designs employing Group 2 colors work best with flowing, fluid shapes. More like a watercolor than an oil painting, with smooth, supple textures.

Group 3 (afternoon, firelight)

When you look at the Pantone references of the warm colors we find in this Color Group, you will see they often contain black and yellow giving them a depth and strength.

They may be referred to as autumn or firelight colors, though they go beyond the red and gold leaves of deciduous trees at that time of year and include a wide color range - imagine a clear blue October sky in New England or a jug of creamy milk to get an idea of the breadth of Group 3.

The characteristics of this group are a connection to the natural world, sometimes described as earthiness, an urge to make a positive difference, a strength and determination coupled with some quirkiness - these are colors that are not afraid to be a little unexpected.

If undermined by colors from another group, these colors can seem over-insistent, worthy and rather heavy.

Group 3 designs need to be well-grounded. They do not sit well with uncertainty or instability. A solid foundation, rough textures like brick or tweed, rounded corners and an organic nature will work well - more ancient oak than young eucalyptus.

Because of the warmth and accessibility of Group 3 it can often be the best choice for broad appeal.

The connection with nature and makes these easy colors for most people to be with.

Group 4 (night, starlight)

This Color Group is very popular with designers and architects, especially from Bauhaus onwards. Because of this they can be overused, particularly in our built environments. Knowing more about color will build your confidence to challenge these choices when you feel they just aren't right for the purpose of the space or those who are expected to use the brand.

Group 4, also referred to as winter or starlight colors are cool, clear, and strong. Uncompromising in their intention to stand clearly for something they are the only Group that includes black and pure white. They also include the primary pantone colors (cyan, magenta, and yellow as well as pantone red, green and pantone orange). Many national flags are based on Group 4 colors.

The characteristics associated with Group 4 colors are, as you might expect, strong traditional-style leadership which pulls no punches (think Thatcher not Obama), determination and material or power-based success. They like to shine and be seen by the world though they may dismiss the attention of others, convinced as they are of their entitlement to fame and fortune. When undermined the colors can seem arrogant and inconsiderate of others.

Design associated with Group 4 colors requires strong, angular shapes. No vagueness or gentleness here. Think triangles, points, glittering diamonds, sharp black and white in high quality, glossy finishes. Platinum not gold, chrome not pewter. A black-tie dinner not a potluck supper.

Color Groups - summary

This small taste of what the Color Groups are, and their most obvious aspects is just the beginning of your color journey. Now you are aware of the concept it will be interesting to see how you develop your sensitivity to harmony or discord in the color schemes you encounter.

As a guide, bear in mind that nature is always in harmony. Whether you are looking at a summer meadow in the high Alps or tropical plants in the Caribbean, the native species will be in harmony with each other, season by season.

A visit to Chelsea Flower Show - or any other exhibition garden - is a lesson in the risks of the great access we now have to flora from all over the world. Some combinations are brilliant and inspiring while you may find others a bit unsettling. Again, notice what you notice, every reaction, positive or negative is adding to your Color Sense.

When it comes to creating environments, publications, logos, or outfits, without this natural guide it is easier to go astray and combine colors that, while eye-catching, are not easy to be with and fail to deliver the sense of peace and wellbeing we have come to expect from nature.

You may have noticed this yourself when you return with treasures from your travels and find that the fabulous artwork or ceramics that looked so perfect in Morocco or Sweden seems a little off in your own environment.

Displacement, of plants or arts and crafts is of course entirely possible and can crate amazing impact, but it needs to be handled carefully to maintain color harmony to show off everything to its best advantage.

In recent years we have seen several brands shifting from their traditional terrain (Group 4) to a warmer image using Group 3 colors. This was the move we made with the Shell logo colors in the 90s and other brands such as the UK supermarket chain Sainsburys and banks e.g. Halifax have undergone a similar transition as part of their brand positioning for greater warmth and approachability.

It may help you remember and define the Color Groups if you bear the two main dimensions in mind.

In terms of characteristics, this chart summarizes the main points explained above and can be a useful reminder when you are working through the exercises, or real-life color applications, and want to decide which Group the colors you are considering fall into.

Remember that the risks tend to show up when the Color Groups are mixed and colors undermine each other.

	Group 1	Group 2	Group 3	Group 4
Texture	sparkling, lacy, light, frilly, fresh, crisp	smooth, flowing, soft	natural, weave, suede, wood	high quality, hard, glossy, metallic
Design	airy, fun, sparkly, temporary	elegant, subtle, flowing, graceful	ethnic, cozy, quirky, enduring, chunky	high tech, modern, dramatic, aspiration
Objects	chandeliers, fairy lights, variety	classical, quality, antiques	unusual, bold, clustered, open fires	technology, gemstones especially diamonds
Assets	welcoming, fun, flirty, accessible, charming, lively	Sophisticated, calm, serious, perceptive, self-contained	quirky, loyal, indie, curious, diverse, get it done	assured, magnetic, star quality, compelling eyes, successful,
Risks	unreliable, superficial	aloof, dry, dull, reserved, un-expressive	overbearing, moody, predictable, old fashioned	heartless, dangerous, arrogant

EXERCISE 8 - Color Groups

Take another look at the materials you pulled together in the last exercise. Focus on the pile of pictures that you feel are in harmony and consider each picture in turn. It may be immediately obvious which Group they belong to - especially if for example it is a strong black and white design with a flash of glossy red - but others may take a little more time to classify. You are aiming to sort these harmony images into 4 piles, one pile for each of the four Color Groups.

For each of the pictures, hold it in your hands and look deeply into the image, almost as if you are stepping into it. If the colors are warm, then it is Group 1 or 3. If they are cool then it is a 2 or a 4.

Now that is decided, which one of the pair do you think it feels like? More intense colors will probably be Group 3 or 4. Even if you are not sure, put it into one of the four piles for now.

Once you have gone through all your images, take a breath, maybe walk around the room a couple of times, or leave the next step to the following day.

When you are ready, look at a single pile. Start with your Group 1 pictures. If you spread them out so you can see them all at once, do they look in harmony with each other? Maybe there are some that you are no longer convinced belong here? Move them to one side.

Do this again for the other 3 Groups. As you probably realize, all the time you are doing this you are improving your Color Sense by spending time with color, aiming to use not just your vision but also more subtle senses and your whole body to attune to the colors.

Now that you have done all four Color Groups, is it clearer which ones are in the wrong Group? Try moving them into other Groups and see where they feel right.

Keep these piles in separate folders so you can add to them over time and increase your depth of understanding of the four Color Groups.

Cultural associations

While there is no denying our physical and psychological reactions to colors as detailed above, these can be waylaid by cultural connections. Colors used at funerals or weddings, lucky colors, portentous colors… these vary from country to country and anybody responsible for international branding needs to be aware of them.

You may decide to carry on with your color plans anyway. After all you don't see Coca Cola changing the color of its bottle from one market to another. Or you may identify a color that works in terms of everything else we have already considered and is also appropriate from the point of view of the cultural symbolism of colors.

This is an extensive area for study, and the table below just scratches the surface. As you will realize immediately, an implication is that there are no perfect colors across the globe. So rather than be put off by this information, just know that it is there and bear it in mind for specific geographical applications.

RED

- SE Asia: Good luck / bride / long life (China, Japan)
- S Asia: Purity, fertility, power (India), sacrifice (Hebrew)
- Europe: Danger, love, Christmas, communism
- Africa: Mourning (South Africa), status of chief (Nigeria)
- Americas: Faith, beauty, and happiness (North American Indian)

ORANGE

- Asia: Happiness, sacred (Hindu)
- Europe / Americas: Halloween, religion (Ireland), royalty (Netherlands)
- Americas: Intellect and determination (North American Indian)

YELLOW

- SE Asia: Nourishing, courage (Japan), wisdom (Buddhism), sacred, mourning (Burma), royalty (China)
- Europe: Cowardice, hope/optimism, hazard (with black)
- Africa: Highest ranked people, mourning (Egypt), prosperity (Middle East), bride (Morocco)

GREEN

- Asia: Adultery (China), hope (India), new life, fertility (China), eternal life (Japan)
- Europe: Irish, spring, Christmas, good luck, envy
- Africa: Corruption, drug culture (North Africa), hope (Egypt), strength / fertility (Middle east), prestige (Saudi Arabia)
- Americas: death (South America), money (USA), nature harmony and healing (North American Indian)

BLUE

- Asia: Mourning (Iran, Korea), immortality (China), Krishna, sport (India)
- Europe: Tradition, authority, calm, depression, right wing (UK)
- Africa: Protection (middle East), mourning (Iran)
- Americas: Wisdom and intuition (North American Indian), mourning (Mexico), liberalism (USA)

PURPLE

- Asia: Mourning, misfortune (Thailand, Korea, China), wealth (Japan), sorrow (India)
- Europe: Mourning, royalty
- Africa: Mourning (Middle East)
- Americas: Power, mystery, and magi (North American Indian) Mourning (Brazil)

WHITE

- Asia: Death (China, Japan), funerals, unhappiness (India)
- Europe: Weddings, angels, doctors, peace, purity
- Americas: Sharing, purity and light (North American Indian)

BLACK

- Asia: Wealth, health (E Asia), evil / ward off evil (India), bad luck (Thailand), death (Japan)
- Europe: Death, funerals, brides (some parts of Spain)
- Africa: Funerals, death, evil (Middle East), wisdom (Africa)
- Americas: victory and success (Native American Indian)

BROWN

- Asia: the land (indigenous), mourning (India)
- Europe: Dependable, wholesome
- Americas: disapproval (Nicaragua)

Part 3: Applying Color

Introduction

In Part 1 and 2 you have learnt about some of the ways in which color interacts with our vision, our physiology, and our emotions. Some of this will just be a reminder of things you already know, and some of the information will be new.

In Part 3 we will be looking into the ways you can use this knowledge, and your developing Color Sense, to increase color harmony for yours and everybody else's benefit.

We will look at three aspects of the application of Color Sense

- Interior design
- Branding and marketing including logos
- Personal color including wardrobe

For each one I will share some examples and explain some of the triggers and how they are affected by color psychology. I will also explain a process you can follow to try this out for yourself.

As always, I would like to emphasize that you are at the beginning of your Color Sense journey. If you haven't been through the training, then there are risks attached to making a guess on colors.

But since most of the colors in our world were selected without training in color psychology, I feel that the information I share here can only help. The more you do it the more you will notice and be aware of the impact of color - and maybe you will get interested enough to want to study more so you can give qualified assessments to corporate or personal clients.

At the end of this book I list some additional resources so you can choose to take the next step in your Color Sense journey. Meanwhile, I hope you enjoy the excitement of setting out on it!

Color Sense in Interior Design

A significant way in which color affects us is in the spaces we inhabit, work in, or find ourselves in for healing, studying or leisure activities. All too often I see examples where the color in these spaces is almost random, left to a builder or decorator to decide or a mix and match of pragmatism, happpenstance, and opportunity.

That's fine, but it leaves a lot to chance and the colors in the space might be working to either good or bad effect. This might not matter much in the corner shop where you are going to buy your emergency bread and milk no matter what the color scheme is, but if you are trying to make an important decision, learn, or need to be reassured that the medical facility is reliable (the placebo affect accounting as it does for a significant percentage of recovery) then it makes sense for the colors to be conducive.

Let's explore this by taking an imaginary brief. In this example, we are starting with a blank space and designing a color scheme for an after-school learning club for 6-10 year olds that will help the facility achieve its educational objectives and be popular with the children, so they are happy to go there and feel safe enough to learn.

We will follow a 4-step process to identify an appropriate color scheme for the space:

1. Identify which Color Group to use
2. Identify which colors to use
3. Consider environmental factors
4. Consider other design aspects

Later I will also share two examples with you for each of the four Color Groups to illustrate some of the ways these principles can be applied.

Step 1: Identify which Color Group works best

First consider the most appropriate Color Group for the space. Consider the client, the role of the space and the people who will use it. The aim might be to create a fun, light, approachable world for young people, suggesting Group 1 is our best bet.

Though maybe if this color choice was for a strict Victorian-style schoolroom with slates to write on and canes to rap knuckles - an authoritarian Group 4 scheme would be more consistent.

So what matters is not only the activity that will take place in the space, but also the style of delivery, the qualities, and attributes of the client organization and how they wish to be seen.

In this case, the facility is an after school club for kids and families who want to have more time learning in a less formal and more social environment than they get in school. So now we have more information about the style of the place and the way they want the children to feel on arrival.

Our hypothesis can be Group 1 but we should discuss it with the client and see how they react before making a final decision. If you are preparing visuals digitally you can easily make more than one version of a mockup for that client discussion.

Very often it is immediately obvious which is the right one, even if the client does not have your understanding of why - and going with that can save a lot of time and stress.

Step 2. Identify which colors to use

Having identified that Group 1 is the most appropriate and confirmed with the client that they are comfortable with that choice, you will next need to identify exactly which colors will be present.

Looking back at the physiological and psychological effects of different colors outlined in Chapter 3, you might decide that some blue would make sense to stimulate learning.

We are also interested in creating an appetite for knowledge; a curiosity about the way things work that could be stimulated by a Group 1 orange. By having blue and orange we already have color balance (red, blue, and yellow all present) but you will probably want to identify a couple more colors to give design flexibility in this kind of environment.

Typically I draw up 4 possible palettes for my client to consider. You may want to come up with others and see what appeals most. More energized colors may be useful in certain spaces, while more calming colors might be best in a reading corner.

During this phase of the choosing you will be drawing on your Color Sense and on your intuition. Start with what feels right and then check how it corresponds to what you have learnt from Part One of this book.

Matisse, one of the great color masters of the 20th century, loved to use blue. And was highly sensitive to the amount required: *"one **centimeter** squared of any **blue is not** as **blue** as a square **meter** of the **same blue"**.

Step 3. Consider Environmental factors

Now you need to consider other factors such as the lighting in the space. Is it flooded with natural light or does it need a helping hand?

Since we are using Group 1 colors, have morning light in mind. Spring sunshine. If that doesn't happen naturally in the space you may want to introduce some light reflecting paint, or even - since we are using Group 1 - some mirrors or shiny surfaces. Maybe even some sparkle if crystals or glitter could be used - sequined cushions on the reading sofa maybe? Or mosaics.

To develop your color balance, you don't need to color the whole room. Try working with blocks of colors of different sizes like the example above to see what feels right considering the outcomes you want to achieve.

Step 4. Consider other design aspects

Lastly the shapes and textures you use will be important. Aim to be in synch with Group 1 as much as possible. That means light, mobile shapes like circles, starbursts, and waves. You could use suspended items to add movement and interest. Fun textures like fake fur, sequins, feathers, glitter.

Group 1 doesn't need to head into traditional pink and fluffy territory. It can be appropriate for either gender. What is important is maintaining that lightness of spirit, avoiding somber, worthy, or authoritarian shapes or finishes. Smiling faces, cute puppies or other young animals make sense for this application and Color Group. This is one you can have some fun with and why not involve the children themselves with aspects of the design and implementation? They may surprise you.

We have looked here at a specific example, but the stages are the same whatever the project. You won't always have the luxury of a blank sheet of paper. In some cases, you may have constraints to be considered like that awful red carpet that there's no money to replace, or a permanent feature like a slate wall. That's ok; you will find ways to work around this. There are always rugs and wall coverings. In some cases, you may just have to lift the attention away from that which you cannot change and focus on creating the right atmosphere anyway.

It might be easier too if you take it in stages. Get the fundamentals sorted first and trust that your instincts will guide you towards the best choices. If something doesn't feel right, then it probably isn't, so listen to your heart and adjust as necessary.

For me a very satisfying outcome of developing my own Color Sense has been in creating interiors that work better for the purpose they were designed for. As well as the hospital examples detailed above it was interesting to work recently with users in a Dementia Daycare Centre to define their colors.

CASE STUDY: Dementia Centre interior design

The Centre in question had recently been redeveloped at considerable expense. The last 0.4% (seriously!) of the budget had been secured by the team leader to work on making the environment feel right for the users. As she had observed, having identical doors along a corridor is not helpful for any of us and certainly not for users who might have memory problems or are easily confused.

I worked with users and staff to identify which symbols had both meaning and appeal to them to represent the different room functions. In the process of doing that, I noticed that color also played an important role when they were selecting images they liked. I had deliberately included for example various pictures of jukeboxes in different colors to see what the users were drawn to.

In this exercise it became apparent that the best choice was a Group 1 color palette with bright, clear fresh colors. When it came to the space those using it wanted clarity and freshness with warm, friendly, cheerful colors rather than anything dark, muddy, or complex.

This information allowed me to brief the artist clearly and he painted the areas around each door to improve cognition and reduce anxiety for the users. When I returned for the evaluation research, I noticed that one of the four paintings was not in Group 1 colors. I kept this observation to myself, but it was a recurring theme in the staff, visitor, and user feedback that they were not happy with that painting. They were worried about it but couldn't explain why. Luckily, I knew exactly what the problem was and could explain it to the artist who repainted that section.

Correcting the color issues on that one doorway not only really increased its appeal to the people in the Centre but also brought the four doors into alignment creating a stronger overall impact.

In fact, the staff say they find it helpful too - a recurring theme when we do evaluation research on projects like this. Happier workers and volunteers are likely to have better morale and patient outcomes especially when dealing with challenging users.

EXERCISE 9: Observing colors in environments

Look around you and take more notice. Which environments feel like they fit well, harmonize within themselves? Why might that be? Which ones do not feel quite right? Are there a couple of changes that you think would help? Is there too much of a color - or is something missing?

In the next exercise we will consider this in more detail, for now let's focus on the overall feel. If you have photo editing software, then you can really play with this by taking pictures of the space and seeing the impact of changing the color of key elements. Try showing your before and after pictures to someone who doesn't know about this work and see how they react - another valuable way to build your Color Sense.

Interior design examples

Let's look at some of the retail and office environments you may have come across, and how they are getting their colors and interior design right – or not.

Group 1: celebration of flirty fun

Victoria's Secret have got this Color Group nailed, especially with their youth brand PINK.

The heavy use of pink, sparkling lights and that fluffy feathery sequin extravaganza is not to everybody's taste - but it works well for the target market. This thorough application of a design brief enables PINK to create a sense of stepping into a different world - just part of the retail magic that keeps them growing with new stores opening all over the world.

The underlying message is that through buying these products you too will become the flirty, sexy girl that everyone is attracted to. Product names like the 'Date Bra', the use of a traditional US university typeface and cheeky slogans emphasize the youth aspect.

Group 1: lightheartedness in a serious setting

While developing artworks for a children's hospital in Baku, Azerbaijan, I had a pretty good hunch about what would be the right Color Group for the children's play area. Although these children have serious health conditions and are brought from all over the country for treatment, they are still children and still enjoy a bit of fun when they can.

First an interpreter helped me run focus groups with the children to check out which colors and shapes they were attracted to.

Then a group of local artists and architecture students, under the guidance of artist Patricio Forrester created the curvy number-themed murals and play shapes over a period of just three weeks for workshops, creative development, and production. Materials supply and budget were limited so not all the vinyl colors are exactly Group 1, but the overall effect is warm and light with a sense of fun that was lacking.

The children were drawn to the joyfulness of the space and immediately started interacting with each other and the space in a way we had not seen previously.

Group 2 for quiet reassurance

In a surgical environment, clients are looking for reassurance and peace of mind. They hope for immaculate attention to detail and high quality finishes so they feel that similar care and attention will be paid to them and their medical needs.

There is an emphasis on smooth surfaces and flowing curves – this can be reflected in the furniture and fit-out. Colors like lavender and cornflower blue, classic Group 2 colors, are calm and thoughtful. Not the place for flashiness or a highly stimulating environment, the role of this interior is to make the client feel that they are in safe, professional hands.

Group 2 for understated luxury

Stores retailing Group 2 type of furniture and home accessories play to the idea of 'old money'. That those choosing this look have no need to show off but rather make their choice based on an appreciation of fine fabrics, craftsmanship and classical designs.

Despite being in a modern house, an interior can include touches reflecting Group 2 colors, textures, and shapes. Features like softly flowing curtains, classic shapes, and a pale floor work well. Gentle walls might be a pale sage green.

Curves of the silk lampshades and chair backs soften the room,
Creating a sense of elegance and grace not high drama.

A more fluid arrangement of fresh flowers is the perfect
complement, though a creamy orchid also works.

Group 3 for robust nature

A Range Rover showroom used a Group 3 color scheme
including the use of lots of wood. They bring attention to a solid
foundation with a large compass design on the floor. As well as
alluding to the adventurous life in store for the future owner of
this vehicle.

The dark green, terracotta and cream color scheme of the
compass is spot on. Now imagine the cream in the compass was
white instead. Can you sense how that would change the feel of
the whole thing? It would sit less comfortably with the other
colors and by undermining them could make them feel heavy.

This can happen too when lighting sources are pure white.
Switching to a light cream would create a more supportive
environment.

Group 3 for quirky innovation

Not all Group 3 environments have to stick to such an earthy interpretation of color. Remember there are millions of colors in each Color Group so there is plenty of choice.

In a high tech office environment, lighter, more fun colors in the spectrum can be used to good effect, along with – in one example I have seen for a company that develops computer games - the visual joke of pixelated objects - a nod to the early days of the gaming industry.

Rounded rectangles on furniture and fittings are perfectly in tune with Group 3 design shapes.

Group 4 for a bank that means business

It is years now since First Direct launched in the UK with an entirely different marketing approach to other banks targeting individual customers, but the design style and branding has been consistent throughout.

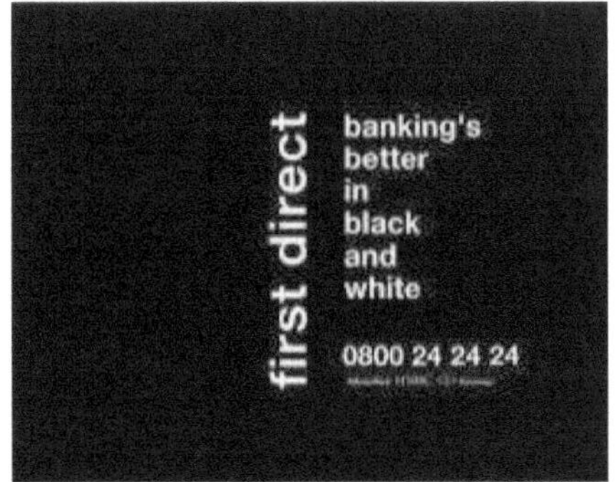

They created a virtual bank with their modern, no-nonsense approach in a world where most competitor banks were still maintaining their aloof expert position. First Direct have stuck to their clear black / white / red color palette and behaved like leaders (the name supports this) even when they were first starting out. Their confidence, innovation and leadership inspire trust and loyalty among their customer base, and they attracted many younger customers who liked the idea of a clear, fresh approach. They made it cool to bank with them.

In recent years the HSBC logo appears alongside their branding since they took over the Midland Bank who had originally set up the First Direct brand for online and telephone banking customers. Luckily both the color and shape of the HSBC logo is in tune with Group 4 so consistency can be maintained. There is excellent harmony in the color palette, design style and brand personality.

Group 4 for high quality, luxury, and excellence

The luxury sports car showroom is a good place to look for a classic Group 4 color scheme. High quality gloss finishes and white metals abound with hard smooth lines and sharp angles. Frequent colors are black, white, gunmetal grey and bright red. In the case of Ferrari and Porsche a Group 4 yellow is also used. Metallics are silver or chrome not gold and there won't be a frill or a flowery cushion anywhere in sight.

Shapes are predominantly straight-edged though some grand curves may also be used - more akin to the Coliseum than a winding country path. Entirely in tune with their positioning of selling cars for proud winners.

EXERCISE 10 - improving environments

As you are out and about over the next few days, keep a weather eye out for environments. They could be shops, offices, reception areas, railway station waiting rooms. In each case give yourself an imaginary brief. Consider the purpose of the space and the intent for its users.

What happens here? Do people need to be stimulated? Calmed down? Intrigued? Reassured? Disciplined? Decide which Color Group feels right to you and consider if the space currently fits with that or has gone in another direction.

Now let's imagine you have some choice and can improve the space by following the steps below. Of course, without the full training in color psychology this will be an inspired guess but the more you work with your instincts and pay attention to all your senses, not just your vision, the better you are going to get at this.

You might not get it right 100% of the time but you will almost certainly improve on the outcomes of someone who hasn't read this book and put some energy into their Color Sense.

The more you practice, the more skill you incorporate into your Color Sense.

Process Steps to develop a color palette for interior design

- Identify which Color Group feels the most appropriate
- Think of 2 or 3 base colors that need to be present to achieve the objectives of the space in terms of the psychological effects we considered in Chapter 3.
- Choose shades of your base colors that you feel belong to the Color Group you chose in step 1.
- Consider the color balance. Do you need to add a little of another color or two to ensure a balanced and harmonious color mix for the space? What feels like the right ratios? Try some color square combinations to see if there is an obvious winner.
- Now you have the general idea of colors, consider environmental aspects - which corners need brightening up? Warming up? Calming down?
- If it's a domestic setting you are considering, then online paint store apps often give you the opportunity to play with 1000s of colors and their combinations. It's a good chance to practice what you have learned. See if you can create four living rooms that represent one each of the four Color Groups and print them out as a reminder.

Color Sense in branding / logos

The rationale

Many of the times I have been asked for color advice it has been in the context of developing or revising corporate or product brands.

Every company aims for a logo that is shorthand for their promise to the consumer. They hope it will communicate what they stand for and stay in the customer's mind. The logo may often be part of something else like packaging, a website, or a leaflet but in many situations, it may have to stand alone for the brand it represents.

And although there are now numerous 'get a logo for $5' web services available, the real value of a logo comes from a process that starts at the heart of the organization, the values of the people who work there and the reputation it is trying to build. Consider these comments from industry experts before dismissing the need to take color seriously in branding and communications:

- *Color increases brand recognition by up to 80 percent*

  Source: University of Loyola, Maryland study

- *Research reveals all human beings make a subconscious judgment about a person, environment, or item within 90 seconds of initial viewing and that between 62% and 90% of that assessment is based on color alone.*

Source: Institute for Color Research

- *When asked to approximate the importance of color when buying products, 85% think that color accounts for more than half among the various factors important for choosing products*

Source: Seoul International Color Expo 2004

- *73% of purchasing decisions are now made in-store (or online). Consequently, catching the shopper's eye and conveying information effectively are critical to successful sales.*

Source: The Henley Centre

Evolutionary biology made sure we registered color quickly to decide how to respond and survive. In contemporary society, market research indicates that over 80% of visual information we take in is related to color – it identifies a product or company, as well as the quality of the merchandise offered. 93% say they put most importance on visual factors when purchasing products. Hearing, touch, and smell account for a total of less than 10%. Of course, this is only a valuable exercise if the logo and its colors authentically represent the organization behind them.

"The only requirement of a symbol is that it have substance underneath: The first thing to do is to try to establish the substance. The style comes after the substance. Only then can the style help the substance, and vice versa."

Wally Olins, brand guru

So, if we assume for now that color does matter in graphic design and the development of a brand identity – including logos, packaging, marketing materials, websites, apps and social media - then let's have a look at how can we go about getting it right for our own products or when we are advising others.

Process Steps for branding

In the same way as in the previous section we considered the purpose and function of the space for which we were identifying colors, in branding we must first consider the purpose of the organization and make sure the colors are sending the right messages.

1. An important first step then is to have a profound discussion with the client. Not just about the practical aspects of their brand - what the firm does, how it is better than alternatives, what its competitors look like - but also the emotional ones. What kind of relationship do they want to have with their clients and prospective clients? Is this a brand that needs to have a lot of authority? Be very approachable? Look contemporary and courageous in its

challenge of the status quo? Blend in with the crowd or stand out? Appeal to a particular target group or across a broad spectrum? These kinds of questions will help you define which of the Color Groups feels right for the brand.

2. Now do a competitor review. Search for companies offering similar or alternative products or services. Pay special attention to those brands aiming at a similar target market to your client. It can help if you represent their colors in blocks to get a sense of what is going on. In this example we have looked at competitors as part of the research process for a new brand called People's Energy that will focus on renewable sources and ethical practices.

3. The first step is to see what color schemes competitors are using. Create a diagram where each rectangle represents a single competitor and the color blocks show which colors are primarily used in the logo. The size of the block reflects the color ratios.

4. After researching all the logos, look for groupings and consider their positioning to build a picture of how the marketplace is segmented.

5. Depending on your client's marketing strategy it may make more sense to fit in with others (familiar, comfortable, more easily accepted but not with a strong personality) or to aim to stand out (distinctive, memorable but takes more investment to establish in consumers' minds).

6. As you work through the competitor brands you will probably find some clusters emerging. In this energy provider example, we saw four main groupings arise.

   a) **Traditional, scientific.** This first cluster tends to be Western European brands with a history of science and technology and a reputation for calm strategic thinking.

Navy blue, grey, white abound. Their logos are complex and with many interlocking curves. Their colors, shape and message imply that energy is a complex business and you need an experienced brand that you can trust to get it right.

b) **Traditional, power.** The second group was also traditional and based more on the idea of power and lightning. They use a lot of angular shapes in their logos giving a more dynamic feel. More gold, warmth, and reliable brown support this positioning.

c) **Contemporary, green.** More recently developed brands have jumped on the environmental bandwagon and are making the most of that association to attract customers who would like to 'do the right thing'. They use a lot of green to communicate this value.

d) **Contemporary, consumer.** Those in the last group, focus on the customer as the hero of the transaction. They often choose modern color combinations like orange and blue or purple with yellow. Their logos tend to be more rounded and friendly.

Notice also what Color Groups you feel these competitor brands are in, bearing in mind that they may not be consistent to one Color Group. For instance, some contemporary logos have an uncomfortable mix of Group 1 and Group 4. You might see examples where black jars against other colors? If instead of black they used, say, a strong dark green, it could have done the same job without undermining the brand.

Of course, it matters less what your competitors are doing than what you want to achieve for the brand you are working on, but this exercise will probably develop your thinking and create a rationale for your recommendation.

So if, for example, you were developing a new brand for high street banking, you might start by ignoring all the existing competitors on the basis that the way this new brand is going to do banking is so different that the existing competitors are irrelevant except as input to create a distinctive color palette avoiding all existing combinations. In the case of logos, you may also have some practical considerations, such as the way it is going to be reproduced e.g. will it be printed on fabric clothing labels or reproduced on building materials as well as the more usual stationery and web applications.

Give your client some options. Having decided on a core selection of maybe 6-10 colors that will be the corporate color palette, think about alternatives to present to the client depending on what they want to emphasize more e.g. their fast service, openness, or authority.

In the following case studies on branding, I will share with you some pairs of brands in different sectors, comparing the attributes they demonstrate - for better or for worse - with their branding and the consequences of their color choices.

It can be a valuable learning experience to take pairs of competing brands and consider the impact of the color choices made. The examples I explain below will give you the idea - I'm sure you can do plenty more of your own over the next few days.

Brand Case 1: family size chocolate bars

Psychological impact

In this segment of the chocolate market, chocolate is about comfort (compared to say an energy boost or a convenient meal replacement in the chocolate snack market). Appropriate colors are those evoking indulgence, luxury, and pampering.

Successful shapes are fluid – the packaging strokes the customer in the same way that the chocolate promises to.

Relevant colors

Tones including orange stimulate appetite and get those taste buds going in anticipation while high status 'royal' colors like gold and purple supported by tactile, quality packaging convey luxury. The brands compared here both use colors that support the color psychology of a tasty treat.

Cadbury's Milk Tray was launched in 1915 and the firm cemented its relationship with purple over decades. Those who have grown up with Cadbury's will have a clear association between this color and chocolate – based on years of exposure to the combination. "Owning" a color like this is a strong property for any company and one to be used to full advantage.

Color harmony

The colors used on a Galaxy (Dove in some countries) bar are in smooth harmony with each other – which is in keeping with Galaxy messaging "why have cotton when you can have silk?" "Silkier feel" and the smooth caressing voices used in their TV advertising. All the colors are in Group 3 - a warm, inviting Color Group with strength and depth that is fitting for the product category.

The distinctive Cadbury's purple benefits from years of consistent use and the original use of purple by royalty (in fact only members of royalty were allowed access to purple dye in the Middle Ages). However, the combination with white and the practical shift to sealed plastic packaging rather than paper and foil does interfere with the effect – as do the incompatible colors used for the health information and some of the flavor varieties. By using white and purple the packaging gives conflicting messages about value and quality – at the risk of undermining both.

Increasing the amount of gold on the packaging would help, as would using cream in place of white. Although the practical and hygiene benefits of plastic packaging are clear, switching to a silk finish would be more appropriate for the category and allow Cadbury to build on their extensive heritage with the British people.

Customer view (based on internet reviews)

'There's something about the Galaxy wrapper that screams out a seductive bar filled with naughty cream'

'Cadbury has got to be one of the most recognizable food brands in Britain, and it's not just the name - the packaging is almost iconic - that shade of purple tempting you from the supermarket shelf echoes right back into your childhood.'

Brand Case 2: energy drinks

Psychological impact

Red Bull and Lucozade are both about quenching thirst while giving you an energy boost. The style of typeface and design in both cases aims for high impact and a sense of strength.

Relevant colors

Orange is a good color for stimulating appetite, and lighter colors feel more refreshing.

Both products make use of red – a high energy color and the color that in physiological terms is seen first by the eye – hence its strong impact. Because red increases heart rate, it creates a sense of urgency which is fitting for a drink that you can grab and use for a fast energy boost.

Using silver adds modernity and a sense of contemporary design. Strong and clear typefaces and designs help buyers to quickly identify their product on the shelf.

Lucozade is a traditional UK brand that has been around since 1927 and resisted attempts by US brand Gatorade to penetrate the market with a similar product. Originally sold as a drink for convalescents, it has successfully repositioned itself for sports and energy. The orange color of the product, reminiscent of its former cellophane wrapped glass bottle has a lot of heritage with older consumers while the appetite stimulating orange works for all potential buyers.

Color harmony

Overall, Red Bull uses a cool, high-tech color palette that can create quite a distance from the consumer. Fans tend to describe its benefits in practical rather than emotional terms. Silver and electric blue give a more modern feel and help carry the product into its key marketplace of bars and clubs.

These are colors more associated with technology than food. Tweaking the yellow circle behind the bulls to a more acid yellow would be in keeping with the other colors and increase the authority and trustworthiness of the brand.

The shape of the can is also in line with the high tech look and feel – though may offer too little liquid for some parts of the market used to traditional can sizes.

Lucozade is trading on its heritage of orange and yellow and using a strong dynamic typeface to bring it up to date. These are colors associated with food – except the black wave under the logo which adds impact but interferes a little with the color harmony. A strong Prussian blue could work better for brand trustworthiness and achieve the same visual impact.

The shape and feel of the Lucozade packaging supports its accessible position – this is a product which anyone can feel comfortable buying, there is nothing elitist about it. Customers describe the product with more affection and the sense that "you know where you stand" with a product like this.

Customer views (based on internet reviews)

> *"Lucozade is very trusted in professional sports … I would recommend this drink to anyone looking for a safe energy boost"*

> *"Red Bull has just become a cool drink that younger people feel the need to be associated with"*

Brand Case 3: men's toiletries

Psychological impact

Nivea and Lynx have taken two very different routes for a similar product, men's deodorant, reflecting their different brand values.

As an upbeat product range for young men, Lynx has gone for a high tech look and feel, using colors we might more commonly associate with motorbikes or mobile phones. Black does not reflect cleanliness or freshness (which could be seen as important attributes in the deodorant market) – but has come to stand for sexual attractiveness, especially for males.

Nivea on the other hand uses water related, cool colors to convey a sense of cleanliness. Blue is a calming color, and white is the color of purity. Although this is a softer approach than Lynx it maintains a clean, masculine look.

Marketplace and culture

These products are targeting quite different groups. Nivea is calm and does what it says – it sells on practical product benefits and a reputation of trustworthiness. Lynx is positioned on the promise of sex with a long-established advertising campaign about the Lynx Effect and how using this product will make you a magnet for attractive women. Each product variety has chosen colors that are used in popular culture to reflect their positioning.

Color harmony

All the products in the Lynx range tend to use colors from the Group 4 color family – signifying power, strength, coolness, and an uncompromising approach to getting what you want (based on the advertising, this seems to be primarily the attention of attractive girls). For a market sector that has shied away from personal hygiene products in the past, it is quite clear that there is nothing girlie about this product range.

Black and silver form a strong recognizable base for all the products – giving the range distinctive stand out on the shelf. Additional personality is added with highlight colors for the different varieties – e.g. red and green for Africa, red and blue for Apollo. These are still mostly in tune with Group 4.

The Nivea approach is altogether more subtle. This is not about manliness but about cleanliness. Reassuring water-related colors are used throughout the range – whiter for calming products, aqua and mid blue for cleansing, darker blue for invigorating. Most of the colors, and the design style, are also

Group 4 though the dark blue could usefully be shifted to be in tune and add more conviction to the range.

For balance and a more dynamic look they could add small flashes of bright orange, fuchsia or red rather than lilac and jade green. This would bring red and yellow into the mix and give a more complete feel to the packaging.

Customer views (based on internet reviews)

> *"You may feel a little girly but get over it, this stuff [Nivea] is great. As soon as you put it on you can feel the cool calming effect it has on your skin. "*
> *"The packaging of this product [Lynx] is very distinctive and masculine. "*

Common pitfalls in corporate color schemes

The first and most obvious failure is neglecting to pay good attention to the colors being used. Now you have been developing your Color Sense I'm sure you have your own visual catalogue of brands and products and publications where the colors are either not right for the application or not right for each other. So just not realizing it matters is the most common problem.

Let's say an organization does become aware of the power of color and decides to do something about their logo or packaging. Maybe to update their colors because they are no longer restricted to the printing processes available when their brand was first developed (e.g. basic colors only, line drawn logos).

They might use a graphic design company to do that and the options could be based on color psychology - or, more often not since it is not a standard element in graphics design training. The board who has to choose between the options are also unlikely to have been trained in this field, so they are deciding blind. Without any objective criteria the selection often comes down to personal preference of the board members - wrangled by political clout of each of those individuals and possibly by other parties like the chair's spouse or PA who were asked for an opinion, probably without knowing the background or objectives. It's an approach, but it's hardly scientific. And while it's always possible that there is a brilliant outcome, it is haphazard at best and could easily generate competitive disadvantage.

But maybe instead that organization has done thorough work in this area. They have worked with a trained color psychologist and identified the color palette that achieves what they need for their organization. The brand colors, sub brands and colors for publications, web pages and so on are all clearly defined as pantones, RGB, HTML, JAL. whatever color specifications the organization needs… And yet… there are still some things that can go wrong during the implementation process.

The most common problem I find is that people in the organization are still using different colors. There are a variety of possible causes:

- A knowledge problem that the brand guidelines are not explicit, not circulated or not understood.
- A technical problem like they aren't aware of how to set color palettes in Office software (in which case I urge you to develop templates and circulate to everybody) or they have a very old version of the software without full color options.
- A practical problem that hasn't been considered during the color palette development e.g. they have to print on a certain background color for reasons beyond their control. This is something that may require an adjustment to the color palette to take this situation into account.
- A cultural problem that they "don't like" the colors. This requires better communication of the rationale of the colors, including the reasons why it is not based on what is liked but on what works. A chance to voice dislikes and explain why can help - the color psychologist might then be able to help that individual accept the corporate colors by understanding their own resistance more clearly.
- A behavioral issue that staff don't like being told what to do. Of course, few of us do, but in the same way that individual employees cannot play fast and loose with the company name or logo (for legal reasons as well as the obvious brand recognition ones), it may help to explain clearly why adhering to the colors protects copyright and helps build a strong brand reputation.

Getting colors right for a brand and company reputation is not plain sailing then. Which is why it can be a source of significant competitor advantage for those organizations that get it right.

That requires a proper brand development process recognizing the strengths and personality of the brand as observed by staff, customers, and other stakeholders. Then the creation of a clear brand strategy and finally an excellent communication process to engage and enthuses everybody with a stake in the brand.

Once established, a memorable color or combination of colors is a huge brand asset that can get the customer thinking of the product or service without even noticing.

CASE STUDY 4 - DVD covers

I was asked by a company distributing films to train their design teams who were making covers on DVD cases for films produced elsewhere.

As various aspects of the packaging are specific to UK regulations, they had the opportunity to create new designs best suited to the target audience.

The participants brought a lot of past covers along, including various versions for the same DVD where it had been released several times.

Later in the training we started to assess the covers according to how appropriate the color choices, design style and Color Group were for the genre. Of particular interest were the films where there were multiple covers for the same DVD, and we could decide together which were more likely to work from a color psychology point of view.

At one point one of the people at the workshop rushed out of the room and came back with a huge print out of sales figures. They were surprised and encouraged to see how strong the correlation was between those versions we said would work well based on their color psychology and those which had sold best.

As a result of the training the team developed color psychology related design guidelines so that everybody working on those genres where the cover had most impact. They knew now what would be most likely to positively influence potential consumers.

Next time you're browsing through a sea of DVD covers trying to decide what to watch next, you might take note of how the colors of the packaging influence you, give you reliable information about the nature of the film, or seem to be off track.

Color Sense for you and your wardrobe

"Colors, like features, follow the changes of the emotions."

Pablo Picasso

As well as product and corporate brands, and environments that have been designed to achieve objectives, color also influences each and every one of us. As we dress each day, we are making choices, even if we must wear a standard uniform and can only define the colors of our underwear.

You might want to choose to live in the colors that will support you and make the most of your positive characteristics. In any case it can be interesting to be aware of that impact, so you can choose if you want the colors you wear to work with you or against you. I am going to describe this constructive relationship with the colors you wear as being in your Color Power.

Personal color can be one of the hardest areas to work with because of the influences of fashion, past experiences, and cultural associations with color. So, let's explore our relationship with it a little first.

EXERCISE 11 - tuning in to your color preferences

Consider a range of colors and take note of those you pull away from. You might have quite strong feelings about them. In some cases, this can be because of a memory - the color of that school jumper you hated or the hospital blanket when you had your tonsils out. In others it may be cultural associations - 'so last year', or a color that has been hijacked for marketing purposes - pink being probably the strongest example.

Pink has been so overused in the last couple of decades to indicate femininity that it can be hard to untangle our reaction to the color itself from the associations that have been built up around it. And thirdly, you may shy away from a color because of the psychological and physiological effect. You may not want your appetite to be stimulated or to feel soothed, for any number of reasons. All of this is information that by bringing into the open you now have at your disposal to accept or re-imagine from now on.

Before making any rash decisions about your clothes, you may want to be sure that your assessment is right and consult a color psychologist to get a personal color reading and palette advice. I have come across cases where people have been given poorly informed advice in this area and completely changed their wardrobe - only to find that they have consolidated everything into a Color Group that is not right for them. Just because you have ginger hair doesn't mean you have to be a Group 3.

Part 3: Applying Color…Color Sense for you and your wardrobe

There are many other aspects to a personal color assessment considering not only your physical appearance, but also what matters to you, the way you live in the world and your emotional and physical reactions to a range of colors. You may want to find out more and get some expert advice so you know you are in your Color Power and can make confident choices about what to buy and what to wear for which occasion.

As a steer though, here are some common color misdirections that come up. You may spot something here that can be of immediate help to you in reassessing the colors you gravitate towards and away from.

Myth 1: The CEO must be Group 4

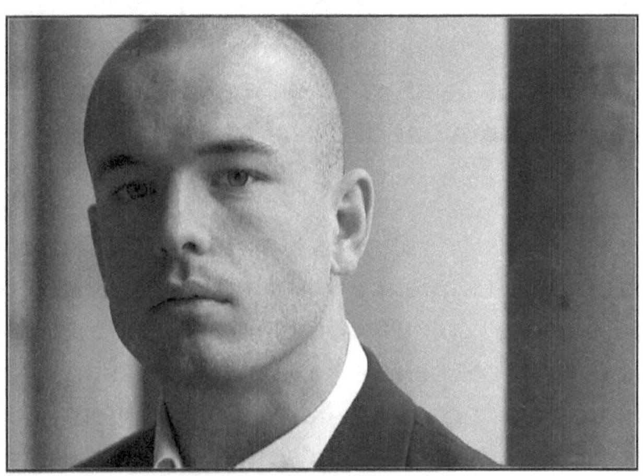

The traditional view of leadership - involving dominant body language, steely glares, and clear orders - certainly does fall into a Group 4 way of being.

Part 3: Applying Color…Color Sense for you and your wardrobe

But the world is changing and so are our views of what it means to be the boss. These days collaboration, employee engagement and good partnering are all important concepts that don't sit so easily with table thumping. The presence in the workplace of more women and less stereotypical male leaders may also have had an influence. And in all but the most traditional and power based sectors (maybe some investment banks and corporate law firms in the financial districts of major cities) we have seen a major shift in the way the CEO appears. Lines have softened and colors are warmer.

This shift towards a more human leadership style does place new demands on leaders, not least that they be authentic. Staff may have practical reasons why they need a job, but if you are a leader and you want the people in your organization to love what they do and put in all the extra commitment and effort that is implied, then you are going to have to be an authentic leader.

That means being true to who you really are, being prepared to show up and be seen. So, getting in the right colors for *you* has got to help. It's not as easy as reaching for the navy pin stripe and the crisp white shirt every morning, but it can be more effective and more satisfying to be in your own color power. So, if you are still in the business garb of your forefathers or your old boss consider the alternative. Consider dressing for increased authenticity by understanding your Color Power and working with it.

Myth 2: 'Real Ladies' must be Group 2

As the Western world moved out of the austerity of World War Two and the rationing and economic challenges that came after it, the 50s represented a new definition of the perfect household. In some ways the old order was re-established, women who had worked - and enjoyed working - during the war, managing without their menfolk or in the Services themselves - were encouraged back into the home and new out-of-town suburbs were built to encourage a consumer lifestyle and offer a greener, more pleasant life with your own washing machine and driveway.

For many women this shift required a reining in of their more adventurous, more empowered selves that they had got a taste of during the war. Or maybe they were the next generation and wanted to distance themselves from that hardship and hard work that they had seen their mothers go through.

Either way, and with the support of a flourishing ad industry, the home, and the women firmly placed in it, became a designed environment for large numbers of the populations of USA and Western Europe in ways that had not been seen before.

Now, a china plate wasn't something you just put food on, and furniture wasn't passed down from generation to generation. The way you presented your home - and yourself as the homemaker - became an important part of your identity and the family image you could create to the world. Watching an episode of Mad Men offers much scope for examining this concept.

Part 3: Applying Color…Color Sense for you and your wardrobe

Part of that shift was towards more feminine colors, especially in kitchens and bedrooms, and a predominance of pastels. In some parts of the market this shifted to Group 1 (spring-like, pretty, light colors) and in others Group 2 (understated elegance, refinement, grace). Those colors can become a habit, even if they are not your natural tendency. Many of us define our lifestyle tastes - the type of jeans we wear, the music we love, the hairstyles we like - as young adults. And though they may shift a bit over the years, it is not so easy to overthrow these influences altogether.

Let's consider then the case of a young woman, raised to be ladylike, demure, and sophisticated. Discouraged from dramatic outbursts or failures in decorum. Let's say she didn't rebel against these ideas and allowed her parents to influence her choice of wardrobe. She is keen to please and to be a 'good girl' then a 'good wife'.

She may spend her early years in Group 1 colors - fun and flirty, the perfect girlfriend and then decades as a married woman in Group 2 colors, politely disappearing into the background when required. Always courteous and a gracious host.

And for a natural Group 2 woman that could be perfect. But what if she is not that? What if there is a steely Group 4 determination beneath the lilac cardigan? Or a fiery poet clads in that pale blue silk jersey? It can wear away at our being, spending a life as someone we are not. It might end up being smothered by valium or regular cocktails or it might break out one day in a storm that nobody saw coming. Less dramatically, it might just be a bit miserable for the person trapped in the wrong projection of themselves.

I did a color consultation once for an urbane sophisticated middle-aged man. He had always dressed in and decorated his house with Group 2 colors. During the consultation it became apparent that he was a Group 3. He wept copiously when I explained this to him and revealed that all his life he had secretly loved drama and intense warm colors but suppressed that for a more sophisticated look that felt fitting to his position. Being given permission to like his 'true colors' came as an intense relief to this individual.

We all deserve to have the chance to be the best that we can be. And wearing the colors that give us our power enables us to do more for ourselves and for the world.

If you wonder whether you might have drifted into the wrong Color Group many years ago, it might be interesting to experiment a little. It's never too late to find your true colors.

Myth 3: Children all like Group 1

Children have perhaps the least control over the colors of their clothing or living space. Take a walk around the baby floor of most department stores and you will see just how strongly coded these items are. Pretty pastels abound and they appeal of course to the adults making the purchasing decisions. Part of the attraction of a new baby is the sense of possibility, of new beginnings. We have a natural urge to see that baby look pure and fresh.

It's an interesting time to find out how your baby reacts to color. It hasn't heard any of this theory, but if you try wrapping it in different color blankets and seeing how it reacts then you will probably learn something. If you have a color preference - let's say, it is light blue - then you can still see how things change if it is a greenish blue, a grayish blue, a cool or a warm shade.

Notice which are your baby's 'happy clothes' and see if you spot any patterns in that reaction. This is a good guide for us as adults too.

Whenever anybody tells you how great or well you look, make a mental note of what you are wearing. Of course, there are many factors - you just had a holiday or lost some weight or gained some weight or had a good night's sleep - but you may also start to notice that some color clothes are working for you much better than others.

So, feel free to dress your baby in the colors that he or she thrives in. They might not be the easiest ones to get hold of - you might even find yourself dyeing baby blankets - but you should find it was worth the effort.

Myth 4: Black is a safe bet

Perhaps the most common misconception in the Western world. Look around any gathering - the bus queue, an award ceremony, a business meeting, and you will see an awful lot of black clothing. It is considered a safe bet when clothes shopping, a 'can't go wrong' stand by and - erroneously - a slimming color.

In the case of the woman shown here, although the dress looks great, it is pulling a lot of focus from her. Do you want to wear your clothes, or do you want them to wear you?

If you are someone who wears a lot of black it might be worth considering your reasons. Maybe it is just a habit you slipped into in the last recession (yes, sales of black clothes increase strongly during economic downturns), maybe it's just easier to stick to one color (everything goes with everything), or maybe you want to look more imposing, more formal, more businesslike? All these reasons make sense, but they are also up for challenge.

And in terms of the alleged slimming effects of black, you may be interested to know that research shows that identical objects are seen to be heavier when they are painted black. Respondents will insist that the black box is heavier than the green one when they lift each of them.

My own experience of Color Power

When I first studied color psychology, I had a lot of black in my wardrobe. Along with various other colors that turned out to be excluded from my Color Group. My first thought was 'but if I don't wear black what can I wear?' It felt like an essential color, not just an option. However, I understood the impact of color much better now, so I decided to give it a go.

I started by making three piles of clothes on my bed. The survivors, the rejects and those I wasn't quite sure about. It gradually became more and more obvious that I felt much more in tune with the survivor pile and just a bit uneasy with the clothes in the reject pile. Not that I didn't like them as objects but more that they just made me feel slightly anxious in an indeterminate way. Quite simply, they just weren't for me.

As I studied the piles more carefully, I realized that many of the 'off' colors were items I had bought in a hurry, or because they were on sale, or because they represented a person, I sometimes wished to be rather than my true self. This helped me sort out the items I hadn't been quite sure about.

Tuning in to my reactions and noticing the reasons for them gave me the confidence to tackle the tougher decisions. But I paid so much for that coat, I wailed. And feel the fabric, it's marvelous. Yes. But… If it makes me less who I am, if it takes away some of my Color Power, then that is a pretty strong argument against hanging on to these regrettable purchases.

EXERCISE 12 - Wardrobe purge

Not many of us can afford the luxury of ditching a whole lot of clothes and starting afresh. I suggest you approach the problem in stages. It can be a bit daunting so why not start with just one thing e.g. sweaters and do those. This will help you build confidence in the process as well as making it more manageable. Try tackling a different type of clothing each week. Maybe start with something easy like your sock drawer.

1. Sort through your clothes and make three piles - the ones that feel right, the ones that don't and those you can't yet decide about. Bear in mind the comments people make

when you are wearing the clothes - which ones get you the most compliments? These are probably your Color Power clothes and gathering them together will make the relationship stronger and clearer.

2. Cast your eye over each pile and see if anything looks out of place. Maybe it needs to move? As with the earlier exercises, as you get into this it will become easier to see how to classify the 'not sure' items so in the end you only have two piles.

3. There might be some items you can happily get rid of immediately now you can see what they are doing to you. Bag them up for the charity shop right away.

4. Then organize the remaining clothes into two different storage sections. Say 'survivors' to the right and 'rejects' to the left in your wardrobe or have separate drawers not classified by type of clothing but rather by those that give you Color Power and those that don't.

5. When choosing an outfit, look to the Color Power clothes first. Then, if need be, resort to the rejects - but at least with the knowledge that you are making a choice. Sometimes you just feel you need a crisp white shirt even if a warm cream is a better color for you, or you might not have had the opportunity to replace it yet.

6. Some items can be dyed, and you might try what I did and get busy with washing machine dyes - in my case I was mostly washing with yellow dye to shift to Group 3 colors e.g. pink to orange, navy blue to greener blue and grey to taupe. This tweaked quite a few more items into my Color Group.

Part 3: Applying Color…Color Sense for you and your wardrobe

My own experience of this process was that as time went on, I realized the delight of having clothes that all harmonize with each other.

Even with only half my wardrobe in active service I had more color combinations and therefore more outfits at my disposal because *everything went with everything*. How easy is that?

Packing for holidays got easier, as did choosing outfits. Nowadays if I go to sample sales or TK Maxx for one off designer treats at high street prices it's a breeze. Knowing my colors speeds up the process dramatically and striding down the aisle spotting a couple of items that work with my Color Power is much easier than having to think about dozens of things hanging on the rack.

Part 4: Individual Color Codes

What is an individual's Color Code?

A powerful outcome of my own Color Psychology training was leaving with a sense of what my key colors are. Not just an idea of which colors would suit me, but a more fundamental sense of myself, as expressed by my unique color profile.

Combined with my experience of working with women in leadership positions, I recognized that this was a way to help a woman – or man, but I especially saw the need for this among women – to understand who she truly is. What makes her of unique value to the situation.

It is all too easy to compare ourselves negatively to others. "If only I was as smart as her", "As respected as him", as young, as old, as tall, as attractive, as creative, as compassionate, as smart, as funny… the list goes on. And it is unlikely that any one individual could ever be the best at every aspect of being human.

Part 4: Individual Color Codes …What is an individual's Color Code?

Acknowledging our strengths – and accepting our less strong areas – is key to finding our true worth and delivering on it. For ourselves, our family and friends, our community, employer, and the world at large.

In my work helping people find their Color Code, I have been able to hold up a mirror for them, helping them feel properly seen. That can be a very moving experience.

My aim is that once they know the 3 exact shades that make up their Color Code, then they can refer to them whenever they need a reminder of just how important they are. And just why they might need to speak up in that meeting or create that situation – because they are the person best placed to do so.

Every good team is made up of a diversity of attitudes, neural styles, cultural backgrounds, and strengths. The clearer we can be on ours, the easier it is to find the confidence to contribute them.

In the following pages I will share five of these profiles. All are real people (some names have been changed to protect confidentiality), who have kindly agreed to let me share this information. I hope they inspire you to consider your own Color Code – to pinpoint the essence of your personality and traits that are your greatest strengths.

Th color recommendations given for each woman can be used by like a checklist. Often it does not mean giving up a favorite color so much as shifting towards a tone of that color that is within her palette. The advantage of harmonizing her wardrobe / home / work environment around these colors is that everything will go with everything. This makes shopping and packing for holidays a lot easier!

I recommended – and where possible provided – some symbol of the colors that each woman could keep to hand. Maybe as a screen saver on their phone, an object on their desk, a piece of jewelry. Ways that in one glance, she might remember her unique power.

Milli

A robust intellect, wrapped in a cloak of courage and fired by an appetite for life.

Milli's Color Group

Milli arrives in the room like a force of nature. Wild curls flying, peeling off layers of complex, quirky clothes. She glows with warmth and zest for life as she perches herself cross-legged on the sofa, ready to go.

The life she unfolds for me is an extraordinary one. She alludes to some of it within the first few minutes… wild adventures, bold decisions, and great success. Many more dimensions of this powerful woman are revealed over the next four hours, as we roller coaster through the twists and turns of fortune, openness to possibility and unexpected glimpses of tranquility that have made up her life so far.

By Milli's own observation, she has lived in Group 4 for 20 years. She can certainly carry off the strength, drama, and decisiveness of this strong color group. Some of the life-stages she describes to me – the toughness of her years in the army, the rigor and strategic insight required for her work as a CFO, her endurance and drive all draw on this aspect of her character. Nobody would see her in a Group 4 color and think she looked drained and tired by it.

But there is more to Milli than this ambitious, high achieving, gritty survivor.

When she speaks of her compassion for her son, her love of color and texture, her craving for uncertainty and new adventures, I see the fiery creative energy of Group 3. These colors, with their complexities, their dark side, their intensity, and their strong connection to the natural world live in her heart and soul.

My sense is that this is the true Milli. The one that has always been there but which she has protected in the past with the shield of her Group 4 traits. Setting out in the world as a 17-year-old in the army she needed those tough characteristics. Her Group 3 soul needed to rebel and find its place in the world. And her Group 4 drive and protective shield made it possible. They have made a great team, these dual aspects of her personality, Group 4 the protector and driving force for her Group 3 dreams and desires.

No longer 17 years old though, no longer alone, and vulnerable in the world, the Milli of today has an impressive stack of achievements: a long and successful relationship with her soul mate, a beautiful son, now becoming an extraordinary young man, career success and epic tales of courage and adventure from her sailing and travelling. Maybe now she can let herself just be for a moment. Hand over some of the breadwinning responsibility to her partner and breathe and expand in a different direction.

Her next chapter - creating an inspirational knitting center and spreading knitting into the world. will require her to draw on her True Colors much more. Not because she can't do the other stuff – she has proven extensively that she can – but because she will thrive. In the more tactile and creative word of yarn she will be drawing on her ability to connect, to build relationships, not only with highly successful people but with the timid, the uncertain, the curious, the offbeat. The spinning of a yarn, the storytelling, the creation of something new and unique. In this world being in her Group 3 will give her authenticity, warmth, and approachability. She will inspire others in subtly different ways to during the earlier part of her lifer.

This new role will require leadership of a new kind. Not based on intellectual brilliance, strategic insight, or efficiency (though of course all of those will still be vital to running the business) but based on allowing others to connect to her enormous zest for life and ability to experiment. Inspiring the courage and curiosity in others, that will allow them to step out of their comfort zones.

So Group 3 is going to step into the lead with its rich array of colors.

Milli's 3 True Colors

Brick Red

Milli has a strong survival instinct. Although she willingly puts herself in peril, maybe even needs that rush, she has total conviction that she will get through, that she will do whatever it takes. Enduring a long labor, surviving the hardships of army maneuvers, battling with the elements steering her sailing boat through heavy storms and taking herself on a terrifying bungee leap are testimony to this. So red must be present in her leadership colors. This certainty allows those led by her to feel safe – her family, her work team – nobody would accuse Milli of being a flake or a quitter.

Fiery Orange

A key source of her energy is her appetite for life. For uncertainty, for adventure, for new experiences. This allows her to live in the moment, to be immersed in the sensations of now. In lifestyle, in food, in all things. So I include orange in her True Colors. Her fiery and juicy engagement with life will inspire those she leads to risk stepping out of their comfort zone, knowing that Milli, underpinned by her red survival capability, has got them covered.

Dark Teal

The third color to include reflects Milli's intellect, insight and strong thinking and analysis capacity. Whatever world she is operating in, whatever new arena, she will draw on this to gather research, analyze multiple perspectives and make up her own mind. Clearly, strongly, robustly. This mastery of thinking processes gives her the freedom to operate creatively, to think outside the box. She can do the math. She doesn't need to be distracted by it or caught out by it. Having the confidence that the numbers are under control and the thinking is rigorous gives her greater scope to think freely and creatively on other aspects.

Milli's Color Code

Based on all of this, I created an image to symbolize the best version of Milli. It is a reminder of her core strengths and the way she can be most true to her own unique power. She can operate in other modes whenever she wants to, but at times when she wants to build trust and access her creativity, this is more likely to be the right channel from which to source her most impactful self.

Several years later a close friend brought me some beautiful knitting wool she had picked up in in Northern California. I recognized the colors on the label immediately. Milli's dream of spinning a beautiful new yarn had spread thousands of miles. See tribeyarns.com to share her wool joy.

Anna

Great depth and universal love, with a strong survival streak, courage, and emotional sensitivity.

Anna's Color Group

The clearest quality in Anna is her courage and resilience in the face of some hefty blows which life has dealt her. Anna is a survivor, someone who is not afraid to take a leap – into some quite extraordinary circumstances. But who does not wear this history as a trophy – rather keeping herself to herself as she cares for others.

This caring side is apparent in many of her actions, busying herself quietly behind the scenes to make life easier for others – maybe without them even realizing. Whether caring for the sick or dying, making cakes for everybody, or trying to rebuild her family, she is always attentive to the needs of others.

Anna is a modest, helpful person who one might easily underestimate, having no idea of her unusual history fighting for causes she believes in, finding ways to protect herself in exceptionally difficult situations

The feeling I get is that Anna could now choose for the next part of her life to be a happier and more fulfilling one. A time when she can stand for who she is, no longer needing to hide to protect herself. A time when she is moving through some of her past, forgiving herself and accepting her strengths and qualities as bright lights to share in the world. Now is a time Anna can risk being more visible.

This combination of traits, plus visual clues, leads me to the conclusion that Anna is a Group 3 color type, with a Group 2 secondary.

Group 3 colors are characterized by their strength, depth, and warmth. The same might be observed of Anna. She is ready to step into this brighter light now and show her true colors to the world.

Often more expressed so far, her secondary color group is Group II – this is a cool color group with calm elegance and serenity. It is understandable that given some of the events of her past, Anna should opt for these subtle colors, melting into the background. However this aspect of her personality can now be safely expressed in terms of flowing shapes and soft to the touch fabrics, leaving her free to live in the true colors of Group 3.

Anna's 3 True Colors

Having narrowed our selection down to Group 3, that still gives us several million colors to choose from. The next step is to identify the actual colors that are the most relevant to Anna's strengths and characteristics. Her True Colors - of her leadership, of her brilliance. Within each of these three colors I identify the specific shade according to her color group as outlined above.

Forest green

Green, the color of universal love, accepting others exactly as they are, is a trait that shows up in Anna's attitudes and the stories she chooses to talk about herself, often operating in service to causes or other people.

The particular shade of green for Anna is a deep forest green, one that evokes a sense of a damp mossy forest floor and magical trees of a northern hemisphere forest. It has depth and strength, like her, and encourages growth. It is in balance, its own ecosystem with no need to be showy or flamboyant. It has a quiet beauty and sense of peace that accepts those who choose to notice.

This is a surprisingly good color for a bedroom. Maybe just the wall behind the headboard of the bed. It creates a sense of safety and being held and nurtured by the planet. Allow the universal love to include yourself too. Just being surrounded by green in nature, either forest or meadow, makes us feel better, and walking in nature will always help Anna feel more grounded.

Earthy Red

The right red for Anna is strong and earthy. Like the red of autumn leaves or a red chili pepper. It symbolizes the survivor in her nature. Her instincts for self-preservation and versatility to adapt and survive no matter what her circumstances.

Physiologically, as we have seen, red raises the heartbeat so it is best used in moderation. The celebrated English painter Turner famously added a dash of red to a mostly yellow and blue painting after he had already hung it on the wall at the Royal Academy. A north facing sitting room may feel cozier with one brick red wall, while a couple of red accessories in the kitchen could liven up the cooking process.

Not everyone is comfortable wearing red – it is a strong statement! Try just a red scarf or belt. Or even wearing red knickers (underpants) on the days when you feel you need a little more spring in your step or confidence in a tricky situation.

Daffodil Yellow

As we have seen, yellow is the color of emotions and creativity. That includes difficult emotions and it is important to bear in mind when using yellow that it tends to increase any emotion you are already feeling as it stimulates the endocrine system.

So if you are already a bit low, a yellow dress could make things worse. Save it for the days when you are already feeling strong and confident. Then it will enhance your powers even more.

Anna's yellow streak shows up in her courage (yes yellow is the color of courage… and its flip side, as evidenced by accusing people of being yellow when they show cowardice) and sensitivity to other people's emotions. When she is in a caring role, it might be best avoided, since over-identification with the person she is helping might not be good for her in the long run. But when she wants to feel her own joy or develop new ideas, then it would be great.

In the home, it should be used in dashes, like red. A buttercup yellow bowl of fruit on the kitchen table or some yellow accessories near a writing or drawing desk would help with mood enhancement and creativity. I don't recommend yellow in the bedroom as tranquility and calm is more often required for a good night's sleep.

Anna's Color Code

It is interesting to notice that Anna's combination – her True Colors are a common choice for flags in African countries – and Jamaica. Maybe they are tuned into these same vibes. The shades of green in those flags, or indeed the reggae colors or traffic lights, are however different. Anna's green is deeply grounded and stabilized.

Based on all of this, the colors in the leaves of the croton plant symbolize the best version of Anna. It is a reminder of her core strengths and the way she can be most true to her own unique power. She can operate in other modes whenever she wants to, but at times when she wants to build trust and access her power, this is more likely to be the right channel from which to source her most impactful self. The one that will do whatever it takes to get through the challenges with quiet strength.

The croton plant epitomizes the 3 colors of Anna's leadership. Having one or two in the house or garden can be a good reminder – as well as offering the benefit of cleaning the air.

In Anna's case, this combination of depth and courage so that she can relate to the pain in others is part of her great contribution to the world. By drawing on the calm and reflection of her Group 2 secondary to recharge when she needs it, she allows the strength of her primary Color Group to become visible.

Mary

A context of universal love, an interest in nurturing and bringing out the best in people, backed up by a sharp mind

Mary's Color Group

The most shining quality in Mary is her generosity of spirit and care – certainly for those whom she deems worthy of such care. She will fight for them and support them with whatever it takes, using her arsenal of intelligence, wit, charm and not a little cunning.

Her flashing blue eyes, bubbly personality and bobbing curls, all indicative of Group 1 may throw you off the scent, however. This is often Mary's presented persona, especially in social situations or with new people. It oils the wheels of social interaction and puts everyone at their ease. An appealing format for others - and for Mary herself.

This frontline player can conceal her deeper, more thoughtful primary color group, the one that fights for her students, her family members, and her friends. The one that is at its strongest when others need her most.

Mary's color psychology assessment showed aspects of all four Color Groups in her personality – as is true for most people. However, Group 2 colors edge into the lead, based on her values and attitude to life – a fact confirmed by a physical assessment. You may remember that Group 2 colors are characterized by their calmness, elegance, and depth. The same might be observed of Mary.

Often more visible, Mary's secondary color group is Group 1 – this is a warm color group with lightness and fun side that can make Group 2, with its possibility of appearing aloof, much more accessible. This is important when selecting Mary's colors from Group 2– aiming for the lighter and brighter options within the range rather than the more pastel, greyer options.

Mary's 3 True Colors

Having narrowed our selection down to Group 2, that still gives us several million colors to choose from. The next step is to identify the actual colors that are the most relevant to Mary's strengths and characteristics. The colors of her leadership, of her brilliance. Within each of these three colors we then identify the specific shade according to her color group as outlined above.

Sage Green

Once she has decided they are worthy of her support, Mary is very ready to find the best in others – and bring out the best in them, especially members of her family and her students at work. She is a loyal friend, a stalwart family member and a trusted colleague. Green, the color of universal love, accepting others as they are, is a trait that shows up again and again in her actions and the stories she chooses to tell about herself. Very often she is shining the spotlight on others more than herself, and every story contains a strong aspect of the relationship between Mary and other people.

Sometimes in modern society or corporate environments, this attitude can be belittled as a sign of weakness but there is no risk of that with Mary. Her quick brain and razor sharp wit – plus that mischievous aspect from her Group 1 secondary, make sure that nobody can mistake her for a soft touch.

Soft Pink

Pink is the color of nurturing and protecting. Before we are born, pink is the main color we can see inside our mother's womb. It stays with us as a safe, cosseting space where all our needs are met.

However the womb is also the space we must leave, to go forth into the world. If you have ever been in a room that is completely pink you may have felt a sense of claustrophobia or overwhelm.

Pink is a powerful color – indeed it is the male principle, the most powerful color for men – but it should be used in combination with other colors to offer strength without confinement. A good rule of thumb is 20-30% pink in a room or outfit. Imagine a man in a grey suit and pink shirt. Now imagine the suit is pink. It doesn't work, does it? If we think of pink in nature, like the rose shown above, then it will be a part of a larger green background. Or the pink of a sunset will be one part of the sky, or only for a few moments.

Sky Blue

The color of intellectual activity, insight, logic, fast thinking, and an ability to process data from various sources without getting flustered or overwhelmed.

Mary refers to brainpower several times when telling her stories and it is an excellent foundation for her other characteristics. The solid ground provided by a fluid and focused brain leaves her time and space to also consider the other person or to inject humor and charm as required. Where others might be using all their processing capacity on the task in hand, maybe coming across as grumpy or short, Mary always has plenty left over for the emotional intelligence she puts to such good use.

On a spectrum of intellectual activity from pure theory (intense navy blue) to connection and application of theories to life (sky blue), Mary is at the lighter end. She is an excellent communicator and very able to explain ideas clearly and vividly to her students. The clarity and openness of sky blue is the color of this aspect of intelligence.

Mary's Color Code

Based on all of this, I created an image to symbolize the best version of Mary. It is a reminder of her core strengths and the way she can be most true to her own unique power. She can operate in other modes whenever she wants to, but at times when she wants to build trust and access her power, this is more likely to be the right channel from which to source her most impactful self. The one that will do whatever it takes to win over a reluctant student or uncertain family member.

In Mary's case, this combination of depth and lightness, steadfastness, and wit, is the source of her strength. By drawing on the lighter, more interactive aspects of her Group 1 secondary, she allows the strength of her primary color group to become accessible. She is not the lonely lady wafting through the rose garden with a basket of flowers and a faraway expression. She is here in the world, sharing her skills generously with those who have the pleasure of encountering her on their path.

Sasha

Connection, creativity, and courage. Sharing her skills generously with others.

Sasha's Color Group

Sasha is a hero. Of the warrior poet class.

But you might meet her and never realize. What you would certainly see is a bright, bubbly, radiant person who listens carefully and responds kindly. Such a light spirit, you might think.

"My mum would say I am funny" she shares and *"At school I would be the clown"*. At first sight you would be forgiven for thinking she is Group 1.

And you would be partially right. The warmth, lightness and people centered approach of Group 1 is a clear aspect of how Sasha presents to the world.

Where you'd be wrong is if you thought this was the whole story.

An important clue here is the way that Sasha is being a mother to Felix; a joyous child with a very serious medical condition that allows tumors to develop all over his body. Side effects include epilepsy and autism. So there are behavioral as well as physical aspects of his condition to manage.

This is a life changing situation that most of us have not had to deal with. It has required enormous personal and practical resources from Sasha and she has surprised herself and those around her by just how determined she has been to find a way through the labyrinth to the medical, emotional, and social support that Felix needs.

"I couldn't believe what I could do when I was dropped in the deep end" she explained to me.

This courage lies beneath her radiant surface and gives it a gloss and depth that mere loveliness would lack. This is the fundamental Group 3 aspect of her nature. The side of her that will do whatever it takes. That believes in a better world and does everything she can to find it.

It is this unique combination of strength and lightness that is Sasha's essence and the key to her True Colors.

To have been through such concern for her son's health, and then so many battles on his behalf, to support him – this is the iron in her soul. To carry that, not as a burden but as a privilege, is her radiance.

And despite all that, to find that deep stillness within that gives her the patience to do her detailed artwork and the capacity to keep on going – that is her sustenance. This suggests a secondary Group 2 aspect to her personality.

As someone who loves people, Sasha clearly falls into either Group 1 or Group 3. Both are the domain of warm colors, though Group 1 colors are clearer, brighter, and lighter, while

Group 3 are more complex and earthy. There are also important psychological differences between the two.

Additional indicators that steer Sasha into Group 3 include her love of the ocean – both looking at it and being in it, the sense of quirkiness, magic and possibility that hovers around her creative work, and the phrase she uses of something beneath the surface (Group 1 is all about the surface, not what is beneath it).

I also notice her love of a wide range of music and her view that the unknown is exciting. When it comes to her relationships with people, her focus is on what she loves about them rather than on charming them

Sasha does have the ability to access her Group 1 persona - which certainly fits with her coloring and curly hair. It is handy for social occasions or times when she doesn't feel quite part of the crowd, but my sense is that it is not her true essence. It is a way of being at which she is accomplished.

Group 2 characteristics are often harder to spot in someone. They are more subtle and elusive. Their aspect of deep, calm self-belief means they don't jump up and draw attention to themselves. They are self-possessed, committed to the task in hand and calm. I hear this in Sasha when she is talking about her creative work. And it comes across in her carefully crafted output. There is nothing slapdash or showmanship-like about the way she approaches her creative work.

I conclude that, in terms of Color Groups then, Sasha is primarily a Group 3 personality, with a Group 2 secondary.

I recommend she sticks to colors in Group 3 but considers the softer, more complex options at times when she wishes to concentrate or find peace. As well as the strong colors she is clearly drawn to for stimulation and strength when required.

Sasha's 3 True Colors

The next step is to identify the specific colors that are the most relevant to Sasha's strengths and characteristics. The three specific colors that make up *her* True Colors, the colors of *her* leadership, of *her* brilliance.

This is not to say that these three colors represent *all* that she is. Of course every multi-faceted human being has so many strengths and different aspects. But this combination of these three aspects is what she uniquely brings to the moment. Her superpower.

Aqua

The blue family is the color of intellectual activity, combining insight and logic. If we are in a room, even blindfolded, and blue light is shone, our brainwave activity will increase.

On a spectrum of intellectual activity from pure academic-style theory (intense navy blue) to connection and application of theories to life (aqua), Sasha's True Colors is at the light end. She is working at this bridge point between the inner world and the outer world, giving visual expression to the personality of the creative idea, individual or brand.

She loves to communicate via her art and can identify the need behind the need for her clients. What lies beneath the surface.

Lighter blues are the color of this aspect of intelligence. Her high clarity shade of turquoise is core to communication and the throat chakra. It is about intellect but the kind of intellect that values connection with others over formal analysis or academia.

In the chakra system of energy centers in the body, this color also represents the connection between the head and the heart. Blue spans the throat and third eye chakra. What we think and what we say.

The meeting point of the courage to speak up and the authenticity to speak one's truth. The meeting between our individuality (the lower three chakras) and our connection to family, society, and the universe (upper three chakras)

When there is weakness in this area it may manifest as a sore throat, stiff neck, or thyroid problems. Maybe a rash on the front of the throat.

Sasha is clear in her thinking and has developed the confidence and courage to speak up on behalf of her son as well as letting her art speak for her clients.

The difference between a Group 3 aqua and a light blue-green in the other groups is subtle. Look for turquoise with a lightness, a clarity to it rather than the denser Group 3 shades of teal and vivid sea green. Look for a touch of yellow which keeps the color in Group 3 and avoids the pastel blues of

Groups 1 and 2. That indescribable color where the sea meets the sky on a sunny day.

Tangerine

As we know by now, orange represents zest for life. An appetite – for adventure, for tasty food, for sex… an appetite for life.

Sasha expresses this when she talks about her creative work, her home, and her family. Eyes shining, expressive, spontaneous. She enjoys opportunities and change.

Orange is associated with the sacral chakra, the second one up. It is a color that stimulates appetite (flick through any cookery book and you will see the evidence for that). Combining red (survival) and yellow (strength, courage) it is the impulse to act, to have the courage to fight for what is needed. This comes across clearly in Sasha's discussion of her journey with Felix.

Note that this is a high vibration color and is best used in small amounts in combination with the more delicate aqua of Sasha's True Colors. The flash of a koi in a clear blue pond rather than a domination over the gentler aqua.

Lemon

As we have seen earlier in this book, yellow is the creative force in the spectrum. Physiologically it stimulates the endocrine system, accentuating our feelings and emotions. That makes it a perfect choice for emoticons – the smiley face feels more cheerful and the sad one sadder.

Because of this intensification of sensation it can trigger creativity and innovation. It has a strong energy so use with care – not good for a depressed or anxious state of mind. If you are a drinker, you might have noticed how the first couple of drinks amplify your pre-existing mood. The alcohol can shift contentment to joy but it can also shift discontentment to despair. The effect of yellow is similar.

Yellow is the lightest color in the spectrum, associated with sunshine and positive thinking. Almost all colors in Group 3 contain a small amount of yellow (eg orangey reds rather than blueish reds, lime green rather than emerald green) which is one reason why there is no black, white, or grey in this color range. The corresponding colors used within Group 3 would be a dark blue (like this font color) dark olive or dark chestnut instead of black, warm light cream instead of white and taupe or olive-grey instead of grey.

Her yellow is the actual color of ripe lemons – rather than the paler yellow we often call lemon.

Sasha's Color Code

Sasha's Color Code is therefore a combination of these three key colors, in specific Group 3 shades relevant to her personality.

Aqua: communication, connection, speaking from the heart

Tangerine: zest for life, self-expression

Lemon: courage, creativity, warmth

Diane

Energy, curiosity, and connection. Strongly present wherever she is in the world.

Diane's Color Group

Diane's strong personality is evident from the moment she sweeps into view. A shock of white hair in a spiky crop, eyes sparkling in the frame of her bright blue glasses, a vivacious appetite for life clear from the start. This is her dominant Group 1 personality on show for all to see.

But don't make the mistake of underestimating this charm and vigor. There is iron in her soul and her secondary Group 3 streak has seen her through some tough challenges, keeping her going no matter what, treading her own path despite protestations from others and taking bold steps where others might show more timidity.

Some of the back stories demonstrate this resilience. The unyielding mother who struggled to display any emotion or warmth, the moves to other countries – Diane lives now in Morocco and Germany, though she visits England from time to time too, the "well you just have to get on with it" explanation for any of the hurdles she has had to get over. This underlying Group 3 streak shores up the bubbly personality of Group 1. It means she not only has the creativity to conceive of colorful patchwork projects and reworking her home, she also has the tenacity to see it through and get to the end, no matter how long it takes.

Despite her strong opinions (Group 3), her dominant Group 1 type means Diane is essentially curious and open to new ideas or points of view. She listens carefully and you can almost see the processes of consideration, evaluation and possibly incorporation as she picks over new information and compares it to her what she already knows. That giveaway "Hmmmm….", a pause, a moment inside her own head and heart and then a decision. It's in or it's out. For now at least. Unless new information sheds new light on the matter in which case she is ready to reconsider.

Both Groups 1 and 3 are warm colors – Group 1 colors are clearer and often brighter / lighter, while Group 3 are more earthy. Because of Diane's combination I recommend she avoids the more insipid or flighty colors in Group 1 and focuses on those with more sharpness.

Diane's 3 True Colors

Having narrowed our selection down to Group I, that still gives us several million colors to choose from. The next step is to identify the actual colors that are the most relevant to Diane's strengths and characteristics. The colors of her leadership, of her brilliance. Within each of these three colors I then identify the specific shade according to her color group as outlined above.

Kingfisher blue

Turquoise lies within the blue color family enhancing intellectual activity, insight, logic, fast thinking, and an ability to process data from various sources without getting flustered or overwhelmed.

On a spectrum of intellectual activity from pure theory (intense navy blue) to connection and application of theories to life (sky blue), Diane is at the lighter end. She is an excellent communicator and very able to explain ideas clearly and vividly to her students. Lighter blue is the color of this aspect of intelligence. Her vibrant shade of turquoise is core to communication and the throat chakra. It is about intellect but the kind of intellect that values connection with others rather than clinical analysis or academia.

This color also represents the connection between the head and the heart. Of speaking up and speaking one's truth. Many of us operate primarily from one or the other. And weakness in this area may manifest as sore throats or stiff necks. Maybe a rash on the front of the throat. But none of these are likely to affect Diane, she is clear in her thinking and happy to say what she thinks.

Goldfish Orange

Orange represents a zest for life. An appetite – for adventure, for tasty food, for sex… an appetite for life. It is not only the stories Diane tells from her life that demonstrate this, but also the way she tells them. Eyes shining, expressive, spontaneous. This also means she will move on, when necessary, not lingering endlessly in a less than ideal situation. She is not afraid to be alone or chart her own course, so she doesn't need to stick around if it isn't working for her. There's too much living to be done!

Orange is associated with the sacral chakra, the second one up. It stimulates appetite (flick through any cookery book and you will see the evidence for that). Combining red (survival) and yellow (strength, courage) it is the impulse to act, to go for more.

Bright Red

The color of survival, or reaction, of fight or flight. Red raises the heartbeat and brings energy into a situation. Diane's particular shade is clear and bright with just a touch of yellow. She doesn't need much of this color.

Diane's Color Code

Based on all of this, images such as the kingfisher symbolize the best version of Diane. It is a reminder of her core strengths and the way she can be most true to her own unique power. She can operate in other modes whenever she wants to, but at times when she wants to build trust and access her power, this is more likely to be the right channel from which to source her most impactful self. Sitting in clear focus and then diving for the prize with clarity and determination.

Bearing in mind her Group 1 nature, Diane would do well to add these colors to a light cream, pale grey, or soft beige outfit rather than go full blast on these three alone. Though there may be days when she wants to do exactly that and go for maximum impact!

Part 5: Color Conclusions

Your True Colors are waiting for you

I hope that the examples throughout this short book have piqued your curiosity and shown that color is not a superficial aspect of our world.

Even if you don't have the benefit of being an artist yourself, or knowing someone who can help, a lot can be achieved with a lick of paint. If you are painting a wall anyway, why not paint it a color that will help?

Each time you follow your instincts, pay attention to your reactions, and observe color everywhere you go, you will be tuning up your Color Sense. So next time you hear that grey is the new black you will know that you still have a choice. Do you follow the trend regardless of your gut reaction? Do you whoop with joy that all those soft grays so in tune with your Group 2 personality will also be in fashion? Or might you bear in mind that grey really doesn't do you any favors physically or

Part 5: Color Conclusions…Your True Colors are waiting for you

psychologically - and therefore visually too. After all who chooses to look drained when they can step into their Color Power and look vibrant?

If you work with clients, maybe designing a uniform, or a retail space or a new website, then your heightened Color Sense will serve you well. Maybe you are interested enough to train in this topic in which case check out the Reference section at the end. In the words of the Cyndi Lauper song, *I'll see your true colors shining through. I* hope you enjoy the next colorful stage of your journey

Further reading and learning

Books

The best place to start is Angela Wright's book "The Beginner's Guide to Color Psychology" which you can find on Amazon

Other books are available which address aspects of color psychology

Richard Lewis explains the history and significance of color psychology in this introductory book while Adele Divine's book Color Coding is on a practical application of color for leaders with autism.

Training

Color Affects also offer a range of training programs: see their website for more info

Other Resources

- Hill and Barton's paper on the impact of red in combat sports

- <u>Andrew Elliot</u>'s work on the power of the little red dress
- The University of Buffalo have produced this useful document pulling together various publications that may be of interest: <u>More here</u>
- For more about color meaning including chakra colors, see Sensational Color's <u>website</u>

Support and advice

I have enjoyed writing this book and sharing some of what I have learnt with you. If you are interested in further conversations about colors in your business, environment, or personal life, including discovering your unique True Colors ©, I may be able to help. You can contact me on <u>cmshovlin@gmail.com</u>